# The €uro for Europe

## From national currencies to the European currency

# *f*oreword

1. This book is part of a kit, designed to help teachers explain the implications of the European currency to their pupils. In addition to the book there is a video and a selection of graphics available at the time of issue in French only. The contents are summarised in diaries published by Generation Europe asbl. The kit and the diaries are available to students in several European countries.

2. Today the book, in its own right, reaches a wide audience. Commercial organisations use it to heighten euro awareness amongst their staff and clients, and the general public turn to it for a better understanding of something that will change their life for ever.

3. This document is the third version of the book started early 1996. It covers euro-related events including the outcome of the Brussels' European Summit of May 1998 and the creation of the Euro on 1 January 1999.

4. The use of the information contained in this book is the sole responsibility of readers. PROMEURO does not accept responsibility for any use, commercial or otherwise, to which it may be put.

# $\mathcal{C}$ontents

# *a*cknowledgements

This book is the result of the collective work of contributors too numerous to be listed here. The most significant have been: Mesdames M-O Kleiber, M. Szücs-Welfringer, S. Tissot and K. Hanin as well as Messrs J. van Schil, E. Larue, M. Dufresne, M. Osterrieth, and Dr Robert L. Jenkins, who, through their present or past activities at the *European Investment Bank (EIB)*[1]*, European Commission (EC)* or London School of Economics, are in a position to provide the reader with reliable answers. This book could not have been produced in its present form without the invaluable and proficient collaboration of several teachers at the European Schools in Brussels and Luxembourg, most particularly Messrs Davey, R. MacDonald and S. Gilbart, who voluntarily assisted PROMEURO in improving the first draft. Additional help in translating the original French version into English was provided by Mr G. Hancock and Ms J. Ryan. PROMEURO also thanks Mr Charley Case for his superb drawings.

To those people, who have sacrificed part of their free time to this undertaking, and to their "families and friends" who do not necessarily share their ardour for the European cause, PROMEURO dedicates, as a sign of its members' gratitude, the quotation from P-H *Spaak* which you will find in the Preface.

PROMEURO is also grateful to Generation Europe asbl and to the companies SOFTE and European Communication Strategies (CS). These have contributed actively to the realisation of this programme, which has also benefited from the financial support of sponsors listed at the end of the book.

**Jean-Jacques Schul**
*President*

---

1. Texts in italics are repeated in the glossary (annex 4) which gives simple explanations.

# from Pierre *W*erner: forward with the Euro!

The introduction of the European single currency, the euro, continues to be a source of misunderstanding, to raise questions and to cause apprehension, not only among economic experts, but also among ordinary consumers. For many years PROMEURO, formerly PROMECU, has dedicated its efforts to help the public understand the implications of this major change.

In producing and distributing material for school teachers and their pupils, PROMEURO remains faithful to its mission to familiarise young people with an innovation which, within a few years, will become part of their daily lives.

The euro is not simply a short-term device. Building on the existing cohesion and solidarity of European Union Member States, it will help to secure the increases in productivity and will develop the economic and financial potential that will support growth, thereby providing new hope to our rising generation of young people.

**Pierre *Werner*** *(September 1997)*
*Honorary Prime Minister of the Grand Duchy of Luxembourg*

*"Monetary Union is a question of war and peace"*
**Helmut *Kohl*,** former Chancellor of Germany, in "Newsweek", February 1997

*"..But the EC as it stands today does not meet the challenge of the third industrial revolution or of superpower predominance. Nor will Europe meet these challenges without economic and Monetary Union and a European defense community. In short we can claim important achievements but we cannot speak of real success until we have established a European federation"*
**John *Pinder*,** former President of the Union of European Federalists

# *p*reface

At the Dublin Summit of December 1996, the experts finally agreed: the euro becomes the currency of a first wave of European Union (EU) Member States at the beginning of 1999.Today support for the euro is spreading to countries still outside "euroland".

So why is it necessary for an organisation such as PROMEURO to publish a book to explain to people something that exists or appears to be inevitable?

In the first place the success of Economic and Monetary Union depends on the willing participation of the people. It would be wrong simply to impose a change that affects people so fundamentally. This would be to disregard the results of past referenda on European issues and the increasingly insistent calls for more direct democracy.

Furthermore, we cannot be satisfied simply with practical instructions from banks and financial institutions. The stability of any monetary system depends to a large extent on the number of people who use it - that is the number of savers and borrowers. Without them any monetary system has only limited practical significance. The market in ecu, supported strongly by the financial markets, would not have floundered in 1993 if it had enjoyed wider popular support.

Finally, most of the literature currently available, fails to answer the questions of ordinary people who have concerns about the way in which the introduction of the euro will change their future way of life. The euro is not the offspring of a few politicians: it had several ancestors and is the logical outcome of a long history. Recording the events that lead to the euro is useful to understand its wider implications as a vehicle of further European integration. This book attempts to address those issues specifically and explains what are the potential benefits but also the risks of failure of these changes.

Protectionism and the closure of borders against newcomers are no longer viable options in a world that has become totally global in the way nations relate to each other. As Theo *Waigel*, Germany's former Finance Minister put it: "Global competition is a reality which neither Germany nor Europe can avoid. To believe otherwise is an illusion which helps neither us nor other industrial nations, and certainly does nothing to help the developing countries".

The best means of surviving in this rapidly changing economic climate and of maintaining the standards we have all come to enjoy, is to work even more closely together, both industrially, professionally and socially. Only in this way can Europe remain competitive and keep its standards of living.

Not all European citizens agree with this view of our future. Some have doubts about the promise of future improvements and would gladly opt for status quo and greater government protection. Nevertheless, the progressive foundations of Monetary Union are in line with article 3.A.2. of the Treaty on European Union, also called the Treaty of Maastricht, which states that the management of the single currency will conform to "the principle of an open market economy with free competition". This is a fundamental principle of the Union which has been approved by democratic processes, and it is therefore this concept that forms the basis of this book.

Even if changes affecting society are only indirectly linked to the single currency, they will nonetheless play a decisive role in persuading European citizens to support or reject the single currency. After all, currency is a key symbol of belonging to a community.

It is this conviction that has encouraged PROMEURO to promote awareness of the ecu and its successor the euro. An educational package has been developed, of which this book forms a part. Targeted initially at teachers, it attempts to put together a broadly based collection of information on the past, the present, and the future of the single currency so that people can form their own ideas on the subject and be able to take part in informed debate.

If this book succeeds in helping its readers to better understand the historical significance of the events we are living through in Europe, the high stakes that are being played for, and if it can convince some of them to become involved in the debate instead of sitting on the sidelines, then the effort will not have been in vain.

*" The best Europeans are not those with the finest or noblest ideas who become disheartened when these are not realised. Good Europeans are those who know how to identify the difficulties, try to resolve them and never allow themselves to be discouraged."*

**P-H Spaak**
former Prime Minister of Belgium

# *b*efore the euro

## What is a monetary union?

From the earliest times, the right to issue *money* was accepted as being the sole preserve of the rulers of independent territories (fiefdoms, cities, and later, states).

Sovereign states relate to one another over a wide range of questions. Their foreign policies, their trading conventions and cultural exchanges are familiar examples. They also have monetary relations. The basis of these fall into one of three systems. In the first, the value of one currency against the other is determined by supply and demand (the market); the *exchange rate* floats freely. In the second, *exchange rates* are either fixed or are allowed to move within narrow bands. The third system is monetary union.

Compared to a floating *exchange rate* system, a fixed system presupposes a degree of convergence between the monetary policies of the participating states. If participating economies fall out of step with one another, monetary authorities adjust the interest rates applicable to their currencies or, if imbalances persist, change the official exchange rate.

By contrast, a monetary union implies a single monetary policy and therefore, a single interest rate throughout the union. For political, economic, or other reasons, independent states accept a common currency either in parallel to, or in place of, their existing national currencies.

## Why have a monetary union?

*Money* is the common denominator of commercial transactions. A transaction (purchase or sale) within the same country is carried out in the national currency: it is common to both seller and buyer. In an international transaction - import and export - buyers and sellers habitually work in different currencies and thus incur an exchange risk. When international transactions represent an important part of a country's revenues, it is in the latter's interest to use a common currency with its partners. In the European Union (EU), more than 60% of international transactions were until recently invoiced in U.S. dollars (USD).

The European Union has created a single market without commercial or financial barriers. The distortions linked to the continued existence of national currencies are a threat to the effective operation of this single market. These distortions stem principally from the combination of the free circulation of goods and capital in a single market on the one hand, and the co-existence of "overvalued" and "undervalued" national currencies on the other. Divergent monetary and economic policies of individual countries lead to differences in *inflation* rates and economic activity levels.

These are a major obstacle to forward planning by businesses and prevent them from fully enjoying the advantages of the single market. For example, UK policy to control *inflation* in the 1990-93 period led to an overvalued pound sterling (GBP) and provoked a deep recession. Meanwhile in Germany, unification triggered an investment boom which in turn benefited neighbouring countries. Over the period 1995 to 1997, fortunes were reversed.

Such conflicts, resulting from a multiplicity of currencies, are incompatible with the single market. Hence, monetary union should stimulate the harmonious development of Europe.

### Have there been other attempts in the past to create monetary unions in Europe?

There is plenty of evidence that monetary alliances have been a regular occurrence throughout history. In antiquity, Greek villages joined together to strike a common currency. Later, Rome acquired a dominant position by imposing its currency on its conquered territories. In the Middle Ages, examples can be found of common currencies emerging. This was followed by periods in which local or national currencies gained the upper hand (the experiences of Luxembourg, Catalonia, and Scandinavia bear witness).

Between 1865 and 1914, Belgium, France, Italy, Switzerland and, at a later stage, Greece, joined forces to create a monetary union called the Latin Union. In 1834, the German provinces, under the aegis of Prussia, came together to form a customs union (Zollverein). It gave rise in 1871 to the Münzverein, a monetary union, with the Reichsmark as its currency. It was not until

1948, following *monetary reform*, that the Deutsche Mark (DEM) was born. In 1873, it was the turn of the three Scandinavian countries, Denmark, Sweden and Norway, to form a monetary union. This lasted until 1931.

### ...And in the more recent past?

During the inter-war years, sovereign states came to realise that they needed to put their economic and monetary relations in order (Genoa Conference in 1922). During the same period the GBP lost its status as **the** international reference currency. The instability and general apathy that followed were seen as proof that the international monetary system required strong leadership. While this was ultimately provided by the United States from 1944 onwards, it was absent between the wars. From 1920 to 1939, monetary policies in Europe were based on fixed *exchange rates* and, for a short while, the gold standard. These policies forced countries with balance of payment problems to lower the price of their goods in order to remain competitive. When this failed, unemployment rose to unacceptable levels. Politicians were pushed into a series of currency devaluations, which in turn gave rise to even more disastrous results.

Heightened nationalism, economic ineptitude, errors of judgement on the part of politicians, nostalgia for outmoded ideas, and misguided public pressures, continued to determine national monetary policies. These were frequently nothing more than short term expediencies and were often overtaken by events. Financial divergences between states increased as countries took turns to devalue their currencies in a vain attempt to lower the cost of their goods on the world markets.

It was at this juncture, in 1934, that the users of the international language Esperanto made the first appeal for a single currency in Europe.

*Illustration 1*: "Appeal by Esperanto users for a single currency in Europe"

### Could not the international monetary system instituted after the Second World War resolve European monetary problem?

In the immediate post-war period, the *Bretton Woods* agreement (1944) aimed to achieve a world-wide financial solution. However, it totally ignored regional relationships. There is no mention of this dimension in the statutes of the *International Monetary Fund (IMF)* which disregarded any separate potential European identity. It was considered that the system of fixed *exchange rates*, supported by *convertibility* to gold, would suffice to maintain the stability of the international monetary system world-wide.

In April 1949, the Westminster Economic Conference, organised by the European Movement at the launch of The Hague Conference, laid down a resolution that supported   European Monetary Union. (Appendix 2 provides a chronological list of major post-war events leading to European Monetary Union (EMU) ).

### What were the first manifestations of Monetary Union in Europe?

The introduction of *units of account* into international financial agreements during the 1950s, indicated the desire of countries to coordinate their policies more closely and to encourage monetary integration on a larger scale.

Also during the 1950s, the implementation of the *Marshall Plan* demanded improvements in the intra-European payments system. This led to the creation of the European Payments Union (EPU) within the framework of the 17-country European Organisation for Economic Cooperation (EOEC). The existing narrow system of bilateral payment agreements was replaced by one based on multilateral *clearing*. At the end of each month an overall credit/debit position was established for each participant - how much was to be paid to all the other members against how much was due to be received - and this was the basis for a settlement that involved all the EOEC Member States. This multinational balance was denominated not in gold or in dollars but essentially in  credits.

These credits were expressed in terms of the European *unit of account* (EUA), defined, like the USD, by a weight of 0.888 grams of fine gold. Member States declared a *parity* between their own currencies and the EUA. The EPU therefore gave the appearance of "regional monetary union". However, no real monetary cooperation was involved. It was the era of transferability of currencies, that is, participating countries in a given monetary zone - such as the EPU - had the possibility of using their currencies in transactions with one another, subject to exchange settlements applied to certain operations within the zone.

In 1958, the EPU gave way to the European Monetary Accord (EMA). It adopted the same *unit of account* as its predecessor. The EMA instituted a European Fund intended to provide credit to countries experiencing *balance of payments* difficulties. This was the era of *convertibility* of currencies. It superseded transferability and meant that non-residents could freely convert their currencies not only in the other EMA currencies, but also into gold or international currencies.

### Did the Treaty of Rome foresee a Monetary Union?

In 1957, the authors of the Treaty of Rome - which instituted the European Economic

Community (EEC) - were not greatly concerned by the question of monetary identity. The *Bretton Woods* system had already been given responsibility for regulating financial relations between states on an international scale. The EPU experience had contributed to establishing, if not real cooperation, at least ordered relations between European states. This helps to explain that the provisions relating to monetary matters in the Treaty of Rome did not go beyond coordination of monetary policy (art.105), free movement of capital (art.106), stability of *exchange rates* (art.107), and *balance of payments* equilibrium (art.108 and 109).

### • How and why was the idea of an Economic and Monetary Union (EMU) born?

From the 1960s, the evolution of the international monetary system profoundly altered the context and gave a new direction to European monetary identity.

In 1962, the monetary programme of the *European Commission (EC)* recommended monetary cooperation between Member States' central banks. Also in 1962, the Community's first monetary expression, the *unit of account* (UA), was defined - like the EUA and in the interests of continuity - by the same weight of fine gold as the dollar. The UA was applied to the Community budget and to common customs tariffs. It was also linked to European currencies to establish special *exchange rates* used in agricultural monetary compensatory amounts. But it was not until 8 May 1964 that a decision was taken to create the Committee of Central Bank Governors.

At the start of the 1970s, the instability of the dollar accompanied by speculation and severe *exchange rate* volatility, prompted the quest for a European monetary zone with stable, but

adjustable, *exchange rates*. The combination of increasing divergence between the monetary policies of Member States and the rapid expansion of multinational companies, revealed the inadequacy of monetary coordination at the heart of the EEC.

*"In the absence of reforms to create a truly world currency, it is the use of several national currencies as substitute, but inadequate, reserve instruments, which increases the instability of the international monetary system"*
Encyclopédie Universalis, Vol. 1982 p. 209-213 (according to the theories of the economist **Robert Triffin**).

It was in this context that the drive toward a European monetary policy developed. Its first outward signs were the *Barre* Plan (1969) and the *Werner* Report (1970). The latter is the first real expression of the desire to create a European Economic and Monetary Union.

### Why did Europeans not set up their own monetary system when the Bretton Woods agreement collapsed?

*Bretton Woods* collapsed in 1971 principally because the United States came to the conclusion that the anti-*inflationary* measures required to preserve the link between the dollar and gold were incompatible with its *public deficits*. These deficits arose mainly from the need to fund the Vietnam War. The dollar link with gold had acted as a stabilising, anti-*inflationary* force; once this was abandoned, it signalled the collapse of the international monetary system. But in spite of the recommendations of the *Werner* Plan, the Europeans did not create their own monetary union. Why was this so?

It was because several European states believed that a system of fixed *exchange rates*

no longer served their interests. Germany could avoid importing *inflation* caused by the first oil crisis of 1973 by allowing the DEM to appreciate. In contrast, France, Italy and the UK, like the United States, believed that by allowing their currencies to float downwards, they would stimulate demand and bring about economic growth. Instead of producing the desired effects, these currency devaluations made imports more expensive and fuelled *inflation*. To counter *inflation*, interest rates were raised, which slowed growth. It was not until 1983 that France realised the futility of the devaluation option.

Meanwhile in Germany, the nominal appreciation of the DEM and relatively low interest rates under the floating rate system enabled it to enjoy a growth performance above that of the rest of the Community. The German policy of monetary stability made it the model for Europe. The UK followed a somewhat different course. As a response to the concurrent challenge of globalisation, it opted for a policy of deregulation. In doing so, it not only kick-started its own recovery, but also developed a strategy that others eventually followed. However, at the time, this policy put the UK on a divergent course from most of its continental partners.

At the European level, and following the vacuum left by the United States' abandonment of the dollar-gold parity, the need for strong leadership in monetary policy became more apparent. On account of the size of its economy and its success in maintaining monetary stability it was clear that Germany should assume this role.

# $p$ reparing for the euro

## 1. THE FIRST ATTEMPTS

*What stages preceded the introduction of the European Monetary System (EMS)?*

a. The *Barre* Plan put forward the first proposals in favour of reciprocal consultations on economic policy and a "system of mutual credit"; it was examined in The Hague on 1st and 2nd December 1969 by the six Heads of State or Government of EEC countries. They decided to implement "a staged plan with a view to the creation of an economic and monetary union". They also decided to examine the possibility of instituting a European reserve fund to pave the way to a common economic and monetary policy.

b. Under the presidency of the Luxembourg Prime Minister, Mr Pierre *Werner*, a committee of experts produced the *Werner* Report. Issued in October 1970, it concluded that it was necessary to establish a Monetary Union between Member States and that this should be done in stages. It envisaged reducing fluctuations between Member State currencies, thereby leading to "the elimination of *exchange rate fluctuation margins*, the *irrevocable* fixing of *parities* and the total liberation of capital movements". This policy would give rise to the creation of a European Central Bank and a "single European currency".

c. On a wider front, a European monetary agreement emerged between 17 European countries who undertook to buy or sell their currencies against the USD at rates which could vary by only 0.75% on either side of their *IMF* declared *parities*.

*For what reasons did this European monetary agreement prove inadequate?*

a. The agreement was entirely dependent on the dollar, the reference currency for all international transactions. But the instability of the U.S. currency and the ensuing speculation pushed *exchange rates* beyond the agreed original limits.

b. On 15 August 1971, the U.S. decided to end the *convertibility* of the dollar into gold and to impose a general import tax. Four months later, on 18 December 1971, under an agreement worked out in Washington (at the Smithsonian Institute), a general realignment of parities to the advantage of the JPY and DEM, and to the detriment of the dollar was established. As a result, the fluctuation margins authorised by the *IMF* were widened from 0.75% to 2.25%. In this way, an international fluctuation *tunnel* was created within which all the major currencies could vary in value as long as they kept within the new margins of plus or minus 2.25% against the USD and 4.5% between any two currencies other than the dollar.

c. The *Council* of Ministers of the EEC, working within the framework of the European

Monetary Accord (EMA), decided to reduce further the maximum *fluctuation margin* allowed between Community currencies (*Council* resolution of 21 March 1972 and Basle Agreement of 10 April 1972). The 4.5% IMF limit remained for currencies outside the EEC, but the fluctuation allowed between any two EEC countries was reduced to 2.25%, giving rise to an inner EEC within the outer *IMF tunnel*. Thus the EEC *snake* within the *tunnel* was born. EEC Member States undertook to intervene to defend the limits of their currencies within the *snake*.

d. In 1973, the oil crisis and widespread *inflation* provoked a new monetary crisis which led to currencies being *floated*, i.e. the abandonment of the outer *tunnel*. European Central Banks no longer defended their currency limits against the USD, but they continued to respect the snake's margins, and on 3 April 1973 they set up the *European Monetary Cooperation Fund (EMCF)*. It derived from the Committee of Central Bank Governors and was the forerunner of the future *European Central Bank (ECB)*. The instability of first, the GBP and then the ITL, forced the UK and Italy to leave the *snake*. France, shaken by speculation in favour of the DEM and by uncertainty ahead of the presidential election of May 1974, was also forced to exit the *snake*. France re-entered in July 1975, only to re-exit on 15 March 1976. The European monetary *snake* had become the "hard currency club".

e. In two reports, one by J-P. *Fourcade* and the other by L. *Tindemans*, underlined the problems of reconciling economic reality with political expectancy, problems that needed to be addressed if the European Union was to develop further. They proposed talks between hard and soft currency, i.e. low and high *inflation* countries, and suggested focusing on some concrete ways forward.

## 2. THE EUROPEAN MONETARY SYSTEM (EMS)

### How was the EMS born?

In March 1978, a Franco-German summit held in Aix-la-Chapelle decided, at the joint behest of Valéry Giscard *d'Estaing* and Helmut *Schmidt*, to adopt a more rigorous system.

On 7 July 1978, the objectives of the EMS were defined:

- to establish stronger monetary cooperation leading to a European zone of stability and solidarity;
- to exercise a stabilising effect on the world economy;
- to exploit the combined strength of Europe, important from the economic and commercial points of views, as well as in a monetary sense.

The Brussels European *Council* of 5 December 1978 adopted the Aix proposals and created the mechanisms of the initial phase of EMS. These came into force on 13 March 1979.

### How can one define the EMS?

The European Monetary System was aimed at creating a zone of monetary stability to be achieved by limiting the fluctuation margins between participating currencies and through the use of credit mechanisms between central banks. The EMS dealt with two groups of technical financial matters:

- a mechanism to control exchange rates and central bank intervention in the Community's currency markets;
- the reorganisation of the former credit mechanisms between Community central banks and/or Member States mechanisms that were

originally set up by the European Payments Union (EPU) in 1950 and extended in 1958 by the European Monetary Accord (EMA).

The agreement defined the respective roles of Community central banks, the European Economic Community (EEC) and the European *Council*, or "Council of Ministers". Central to its operation was a *unit of account* known as the European Currency Unit (ECU) which progressively acquired the minimum characteristics necessary to become a currency, expressed as the private "ecu" (for the difference between ECU and ecu, see part 3).

### How did the exchange and intervention mechanism work?

Two reference systems were used to determine the equilibrium point of the currency market: the table of intervention limits of participating currencies and the degree of convergence.

a. Each participating currency had a value expressed in ecu. This permitted a matrix of bilateral *central rates* i.e. the value of each participating currency against each of the other participating currencies, to be established. Around these central rates were fluctuation margins - the maximum permitted fluctuation was initially 2.25% but 15% as from 1993 - and from these margins a table of intervention limits was obtained. The exchange rates of participating currencies were not allowed to fluctuate outside these margins. If they did, central banks were obliged, by the purchase and sale of their own currencies (not ecu), to bring the exchange rates back within the margins. We were dealing here with bilateral intervention, i.e. it did not concern more than two countries.

b. The mechanism also provided for multilateral intervention (involving more than two countries) which promoted convergence between currencies. To this aim, for each currency, the maximum divergence from all other participating currencies was determined. A "divergence indicator", representing the maximum permitted divergence, was fixed for each currency at 75% of the limits of intervention. If a currency exceeded its "divergence indicator", the authorities concerned had to take corrective measures. These included adjustments to internal monetary policy or to *central rates*, plus various forms of intervention.These mechanisms did not prevent certain countries from leaving the EMS.

### How did the credit mechanisms of the European Monetary System work?

All EEC Member States participated in the functioning of the four mechanisms:

● Very short-term credit facilities. Unlimited facilities were granted between central banks to ensure that interventions in the currency markets were possible. Maximum duration was limited to around 3 months.

● Short-term financial support. This was also limited: a maximum of 3 roll-over credits of 3 months each between central banks.

● Medium-term financial assistance. This concerned credits over 2 to 5 years between Member States, normally channelled through central banks.

● Community loans. These were granted between Member States and the EEC, for fixed durations, in cases of financial difficulties provoked by *balance of payments* problems.

### ✐ Did the European Monetary System render national currencies superfluous?

The role of the EMS was not to replace national currencies by a single currency. Its exclusive aim was the creation of a zone of greater stability between national currencies around a pivot currency - the ECU. With the ECU, Europe introduced its own reference currency instead of the USD.

National currencies remained the basis of the currency markets. The private ecu did not replace them, it was merely an addition or a parallel currency which, however, played a critical role as the forerunner of the euro.

## 3. THE ECU

### The ECU: a basket currency...?

The ECU was a basket composed of 12 Community Member State currencies. The quantity of each currency in the basket was fixed. It corresponded in principle to the relative weight of the economy and the population of each participating state. Up until 1st November 1993, when the Treaty on European Union superseded the European Community, the composition could be revised every 5 years. Before that date, each time a country joined the Union, its national currency was integrated into the basket giving rise to uncertainty as to the ECU's future value. Article 109.G. of the Treaty froze the composition of the ECU. This is why the currencies of the three most recent EU Member States - Austria, Finland and Sweden - were not represented in the ECU.

*Illustration 2*: "Composition of the ecu basket"

The ECU basket existed in two forms: the official ecu and the private ecu.

### What was the official ECU?

The official ECU was the name given to the *unit of account*/currency used within the framework of the EMS. Its value was

calculated periodically by the EC on the basis of the exchange rates of the 12 component currencies.

### What was the private ecu?

It was a measure of value used in commercial and financial contracts. Its composition was the same as that of the official ECU. Its value, by contrast, was determined by the supply and demand situation of the ecu in financial markets. Consequently, it could diverge slightly from that of the official ECU. The "delta" measured the difference between the official ECU and the private ecu and provided an indication of the markets' confidence in the future currency. It reached -3% in 1994 but turned definitely positive at the beginning of 1998.

*Illustration 3*: "Evolution of the ecu delta"

It is worth noting, however, that during the

financial upheavals which convulsed European financial markets in 1992 and 1993, the definition of the ecu was never under threat, neither by the official authorities nor in private markets.

### What was the ecu not?

The ecu did not exist in notes and coins. The coins stamped with the word "ecu", which you have perhaps come across, are worth something only as a collector's item. The value of these coins lies in their metal content and not in their *face value*.

### The ecu: how was it created?

The ecu was created by banks via their credit operations. In the absence of a European central bank, *clearing* between credit and debit positions in ecu was effected by the *Ecu Banking Association (EBA)* with the technical cooperation of the *Bank for International Settlements (BIS)*. The transmission of messages was assured by the *SWIFT* network.

The system comprised 46 clearing banks. Banks which were not members, the correspondent banks, had to channel their payment orders via a clearing bank. Moreover, non-banks (savings banks, postal cheque account services) had necessarily to pass through the intermediary of a bank.

### The ecu market: how real was it?

The absence of notes or coins made the ecu seem abstract. It existed in scriptural form only, i.e. transfers between bank accounts, cheques, credit cards etc. Everyone could, for example, open a current-account in ecu. Transactions, in national currencies were also predominantly scriptural rather than fiduciary, i.e. in the form of notes and coin. The ecu market was very real indeed and, in terms of its size, far from negligible.

### Was the ecu money in its own right?

The three functions which a money must fulfil are: to be a *unit of account*, a *store of value* (for savings) and a *means of payment*.

Since 1975, the ECU had been the official *unit of account* of the EU. It was also used by numerous public or private *businesses* (Fiat, Alcatel, Amadeus, Eutelstat, Merck...) to denominate their accounts, as a reference price in invoicing and to pay their suppliers. The majority of European railway and telecommunications companies used the ECU in their international transactions.

The ecu's role as a store of value was well evidenced by its development in financial markets. Numerous financial products were available in ecu: bonds, forward contracts, options, swaps, commercial bills/paper, deposit certificates. Individuals could open a bank account in ecu, issue eurocheques in ecu or have a credit card denominated in ecu.

In 1992, the ecu was on the point of becoming the third most important currency (after the USD and the DEM) in the bond markets. Until 1998 daily settlements by the *EBA* amounted to around 50 billion ecu.

However, the use of the ecu as a *means of payment* in commercial transactions remained insignificant. Unless the two parties to the transaction agreed to it, the ecu could not be used. It is this lack of recourse to the ecu in commercial transactions which reduced its *moneyness*. Furthermore, like most foreign currencies, the ecu, which did not exist in *fiduciary* form, was not legal tender. The ecu was nevertheless convertible into currencies having *legal tender*. In a bank, ecus could be changed into the currency of your preference.

### What were the advantages of the ecu basket ?

● Neutrality.
a. In denominating an international transaction, especially between countries whose currencies form part of its composition, the ecu dispensed with the need to choose between the currency of the buyer and that of the seller. It also divided the exchange risk more equitably.

b. Similarly, an investor wishing to buy European financial assets and wanting to avoid the risks associated with individual national currencies could purchase securities in ecu. This was particularly important for non-European investors, who had only a limited knowledge of individual Member States. Also, many financial products that were not available in some national currencies might be available in ecu.

● Simplification. A company with operations in several European countries could simplify its treasury management, and thus cut costs, by using the ecu in place of national currencies. The use of the ecu also improved price transparency, making it easier to compare the cost of the same goods between one country and another.

● Stability. Thanks to its basket status and to the EMS, which combined to limit participating currencies' exchange rate variations, the ecu benefited from greater stability than national currencies. The latter could be highly volatile in the short-term.

### What were the deficiencies of the ecu basket ?

● Absence of a "territorial base". Without a domestic market, the ecu was everywhere a foreign currency and this discouraged users.

As the ecu was not *legal tender*, no one was obliged to accept the settlement of a debt in ecus. Because some people were unwilling to use it, their trade partners were also prevented from using it. It is rather like being the only one with a telephone.

● Complication of a parallel currency. The ecu was a 16th currency within the EU. Neither coins nor notes existed in ecu. Whilst the ecu could be used in certain transactions, for others it was necessary to turn to national currencies. This applied, for example, to taxes and to most products and services (petrol, energy, water, public transport...) whose official price was fixed in national currency. In the majority of countries, companies had to issue share capital and present their accounts in national currency.

● Exchange risk. In spite of the stability of the ecu in the short-term, an exchange risk nevertheless existed. As a basket currency, the ecu necessarily depreciated against "strong" currencies and appreciated against "weak" currencies. Investors from strong currency countries were confronted with the risk of a depreciation in their ecu savings, while borrowers from weak-currency countries risk seeing their debt increase when converted from ecu back into national currency. Thanks to the framework provided by the Exchange Rate Mechanism (ERM), the exchange fluctuations of currencies composing the ecu, against the ecu itself were generally smaller than against non-EMS currencies. The exchange rate risk also lessened as economic policies progressively converge.

This weak point of the ecu was accentuated by the tendency of certain countries to finance their public debt in the ecu market, a possibility that has now been eliminated by forbidding central banks to offer *overdrafts* to their governments.

To minimise fluctuations of the ecu, the United Kingdom proposed to transform the ecu into a "hard ecu". This could be achieved by, for instance, increasing the weight of a weak currency in proportion to its devaluations. The concept was never made operational.

● High cost of banking transactions. The private ecu was created by commercial and investment banks and was not issued by a central bank. As a result, there was no *lender of last resort* as there was for national currencies, thus introducing an element of risk for the ecu, even though all necessary precautions had been taken to ensure the stability of the system. The fact that the ecu was used only in a small number of sales, reduced its *liquidity*. The exchange risk, linked to a lack of *liquidity* in the market, entailed increased costs on ecu transactions. The *EBA*'s ecu clearing system was only suitable for large amounts.

*Illustration 4a*: "Historic of the value of seven EU currencies (plus USD and JPY) against the ecu/euro 1980-1999"

*Illustration 4b*: "Historic of the value of the remaining eight EU currencies (plus USD) against the ecu/euro 1980-1999"

### What role has the Delors Plan played in European Monetary Union?

This plan, also called the "'*Delors* Committee Report" was conceived by a dozen experts including several Governors of Central Banks. Its conclusions were submitted in 1989 by Jacques *Delors*, the President of the Commission to the European Council in Madrid. It proposed a progressive transition toward single currency in support of the single market. It revealed the need for a new Treaty. It also demonstrated that market forces would not suffice to bring single currency about. It

asked that measures be taken in support of the private ecu, and to stimulate economic convergence. It also recommended the creation of a *European System of Central Banks (ESCB)*. Finally, it took up the principle developed in the Werner Plan of a staged approach toward single currency, without, however, fixing specific dates as is the case in the Union Treaty.

Some remnants of the parallel currency scenario from the *Delors* Plan were carried over into articles 109 F.2 and 109 J.1 of the Treaty on European Union which presume the ongoing development of the ecu market right up to the advent of the single currency.

The idea of a "natural evolution" towards the single currency was finally abandoned in favour of the "big bang" scenario, proposed by the *European Monetary Institute (EMI)* and the EC, and enshrined in the Madrid Summit of December 1995. According to this scenario, the introduction of the single currency would take place in one fell swoop with a minimal transition period.

### Did the announcement of the euro's arrival mean the disappearance of the ecu?

Both the official ECU and the private ecu ceased to exist when the euro came into being on 1st January 1999. On this date, all ECUs were converted into euros at a rate of 1 to 1, irrespective of the countries participating in EMU. Until then, the ecu remained the European currency.

### How important was the ecu to the development of a single currency?

The ecu demonstrated the need for a common currency in Europe and, notably, for a large capital market. The ecu was also a symbol of the North-South solidarity in the Union which is a founding principle of the Treaty of Rome.

Experience with the ecu, particularly during the turbulent times between 1992 and 1993, demonstrated clearly the need for convergence in the economic policies of Member States. Both of these factors were essential to the creation of a stable monetary system.

It also confirmed the dangers when popular support for monetary integration is not present.

The replacement of the ecu by the euro was the last stage of a journey that had started in 1950 with the launch of the EUA. Without the ecu, it would not have been possible to determine the future value of each currency in euro before January 1999 and, in doing so, prepare Europeans to the euro.

### From ECU to euro: what is the relationship?

On 1st January 1999 the ECU was exchanged on a 1 to 1 basis for the euro. The ECU was not a wholly independent currency since its value depended on that of the constituent currencies, those being the only ones to have a *lender of last resort*. Therefore, the ecu did not possess all the attributes of money.

The euro, by contrast, possesses all these attributes, in particular a *means of payment* in commercial transactions and in transactions with national authorities (for example tax payments).

In the countries that adopted it, the euro is *legal tender* and it will exist in the form of notes and coins as from 1st January 2002.

The institutional framework differs from that of the ecu: monetary policy relating to the euro is managed by the *European Central Bank (ECB)*. Its primary objective is to maintain price stability.

The fundamental difference is that while the ecu complemented national currencies and thus did not eliminate fluctuations between them, the euro replaces national currencies of the countries participating in the Economic and Monetary Union. It thus provides much greater stability in the monetary system.

### How could the ECU - a basket currency of 12 national currencies - be equal to a euro?

In the past, the existence of the ECU was not affected by whether the pound sterling was in or out of the exchange rate mechanism of the EMS. Thus there is nothing surprising in the equivalence between ECU and euro, whichever currencies are within the Economic and Monetary Union (EMU).

The Treaty on European Union states - Art. 109 L §4 - that "this measure" (the change-over from the ecu-basket to ecu-currency), "shall by itself not modify the external value of the ECU" (renamed euro).

In fact, on the day of its conversion into euro, the ECU basket disappeared. It is, as it were, disconnected from its component currencies. Since, however, one former ECU equals one euro, it retains its former value against the dollar and other external currencies. The ECU was worth USD 1.083480 at midnight on 31 December 1998, the euro was still worth USD 1.083480 on 1st January 1999.

This allowed component currencies which are part of EMU to fix their conversion rates in relation to the euro without disrupting the European currency. The one for one exchange rate between ECU and euro was confirmed within the judicial framework of the euro approved by the Heads of State or Government at Dublin in December 1996.

To reassure the media and the markets, the *European Investment Bank (EIB)* launched in 1996 an ECU denominated bond (500 million) carrying the explicit guarantee of a one ECU to one euro conversion. It followed this up in January 1997 by placing the very first issue denominated in euro (1000 million over 7 years). The *EIB* also launched issues denominated in various Member State currencies which include an option to convert them into euro at the exchange rates fixed upon entry to EMU.

In the run-up to ECU, a number of public bodies, including the *EC* and the *EIB*, have publicly confirmed that their entire debt in ECU would be converted into euro at the 1 to 1 rate, even when this guarantee was not explicitly mentioned in legal documents.

## 4. OBJECTIVES AND ORIGINALITY OF ECONOMIC & MONETARY UNION (EMU)

### What milestones mark the road from EMS to EMU?

First, the *Genscher-Colombo* Plan and the report of an ad-hoc committee on 30 June 1985 paved the way for a decision by the Milan European *Council* to hold an intergovernmental conference to revise the Treaty of Rome. The text of this agreement, dated 17 December 1985 and known as the "Single Act", was approved by the Luxembourg European Council of December 1985, signed by Member States in February 1986 and subsequently ratified, and came into force on 1st July 1987.

### What were the objectives of the Single Act in relation to monetary issues?

Its principal objective was the realisation of the internal market in Europe by 31 December 1992. The Single Act raised the prospect of monetary problems, and looked to the EMS and the ECU in particular to provide future solutions. Accordingly, a new chapter (Art. 102 A), entitled "Monetary Cooperation in economic and monetary policy", was inserted into the "Treaty of Rome".

### What was the role of the Monetary Committee?

The impetus given to the technical preparation for the single currency and the progress achieved in resolving the questions surrounding the institutional management of the euro (notably regarding the *European System of Central Banks (ESCB)* and the *ECB*), owe much to the work of the Monetary Committee. A consultative body, set up by the Treaty on European Union - Art. 109 C, the committee comprised two representatives from each Member State and from the EC. It brought together representatives of European central banks, finance ministers, and the EC, and prepared meetings of the *Council of Economic and Finance Ministers (ECOFIN)*.

The capacity of its members to contribute to the preparation of Monetary Union by virtue of their technical competence and their ability to see beyond narrow national interests under the leadership of Sir Nigel *Wicks*, has been acknowledged as the source of the Committee's positive influence.

In January 1999, this Committee was replaced by the *Economic and Financial Committee (EFC)*.

### What makes EMU different from previous monetary unions?

EMU is different because the euro is created by sovereign states, each of which continues to have its own central bank. In the past, monetary agreements were one of three types. They were either:

● designed to ensure that each country's currency enjoyed reciprocal freedom of circulation in all the others; or

● concluded in favour of the currency of one country which would then become that of the other partner states; or

● accompanied by a political agreement, the creation of a central bank and the issuing of a common currency.

The administrative arrangements governing the EURO are equally original in that each state maintains a certain autonomy in relation to economic, monetary and fiscal policy. This allows variations in the conditions applied to securities denominated in euro.

### What were the main features of the journey to Monetary Union?

The three main characteristics of the movement towards EMU were as follows:

● its short duration: it took more than a century for the United States to establish its central bank and almost 40 years for the German nation to move from a single market to a single currency. The European Union, despite its cultural and linguistic diversity, will have taken fewer than 50 years to set up a single currency.

● its pragmatism:
as in former monetary unions, this Monetary Union precedes economic and political union. This was also the case in the Scandinavian and German monetary unions. However, it is worth noting that no monetary union has managed to last more than 60 years without the support of political union, and that the *Werner* Plan appealed for such a political union to guarantee the durability of any European Monetary Union.

● its constancy: the transition from the European Unit of Account (EUA) to the euro, via the UC (1962), the ecu-basket (1979) and the private ecu (1981) has always taken place at a one for one exchange rate. Even at moments of serious monetary crisis (1992-1993) the definition of the ecu has not been called into question. Also noteworthy is the fact that the notion of external stability, first developed for the EUA by making it equal to the USD, reduces exchange risks for businesses engaged in import and export with the rest of the world. This constancy explains why the value of the ecu and, hence the euro, is not far off the USD.

# *r*eady for the euro

## 1. TOWARDS EMU AND THE SINGLE CURRENCY

### Why have a single currency?

a. History has shown that in Europe, monetary systems based on national currencies and exchange controls have not been able to guarantee lasting stability. At the same time the full potential of the European economy has not been exploited. Individual countries have been preoccupied with competing against each other, rather than cooperating together for the good of the whole. A continuous series of economic crises in Europe bears witness to this. The single currency will provide greatly increased economic cooperation and coordination, so making it an economic as well as a Monetary Union. Hence the "E" in "EMU".

b. At the international level, experience has shown that using one country's currency to anchor the international monetary system does not guarantee stability in the long term. Sooner or later, the particular interests of the country in question diverge from, and take precedence over, the interests of the international community. The euro progressively eliminates the risk arising from the current use of the dollar in a large proportion of commercial transactions both within the Union and with the outside world. It will serve as an example of how to establish a common currency between countries that have common aims.

c. The elimination of exchange fluctuations within Europe and the emergence of a European currency leads to a fundamental change in global monetary relations. These will henceforth be based on just three international currencies: the dollar, the yen and the euro.

d. Realising the full potential of the European single market enhances the Union's economic development. This is done principally through the elimination of unnecessary costs and distortions arising from exchange risks between national currencies. Sound monetary and budgetary discipline reinforces price stability. It eliminates the possibility of competitive devaluations or over-valuations between EMU members and, as a result of low and stable interest rates, stimulates economic growth and employment.

e. To provide Europe with a political status that has a truly international dimension. Take an absurd example: how important would the United States be if there existed a Texan dollar, an Alabaman dollar, an Oregon dollar, etc... ? It would certainly not enjoy the benefit of a world currency symbolised by the USD. With the euro, Europe will become a political reality with its own common *unit of account*, *store of value*, and *means of payment*.

f. To better protect the European identity and that of the countries whose cultures contribute to the uniqueness of the European Union.

*"Europe will have its single currency or it will not be Europe"*

**J. Rueff**
former President of the
Bank of France

The single currency is the way towards lasting economic, as well as monetary integration in Europe.

### Is the movement towards EMU irreversible?

The Treaty on European Union, also called the "Maastricht Treaty" after the name of the Dutch town where it was signed, was ratified in 1993 by the normal democratic processes in **all** Member States. It stipulated that EMU would take place. On this there was no going back. The protocol (no. 10) on the transition to the third stage of EMU specifies: "The high contracting parties declare the irreversible character of the Community's movement to the third stage of Economic and Monetary Union". Only three countries: the United Kingdom, Denmark and Sweden have an exemption (opt-out) clause.

Note that the Maastricht Treaty covers more than explicitly economic matters. Hence the European Economic Community (EEC) instituted by the Treaty of Rome has now become the European Union (EU).

### What measures are being taken to get there?

Recent progress towards the single currency has been considerable:

The main stages have been the following:
July 1990: Single Act. Since 1957 the recommendations of the Treaty of Rome concerning the opening up of capital markets had failed to have any great effect.

However, thanks to the Single Act, such liberalisation was now taking place in the majority of Member States. Thus began Stage 1 of the movement towards EMU.

1992 and 1993: Referenda in Denmark and France revealed a lack of popular support for the European monetary integration process. Those in public office came to realise the importance of mobilising citizens' involvement in European integration.

The German Constitutional Court decided that the government would have to obtain parliamentary approval for Germany's participation.

January 1994: Beginning of Phase II. Creation of the European Monetary Institute (EMI), with headquarters in Frankfurt. This was the precursor of the future *European Central Bank* which manages the single currency as of its introduction.

December 1995, Madrid Summit: Redefinition of the name of the single currency as the euro and acceptance of the timetable for its adoption in 1999.

December 1996, Dublin Summit: Acceptance of the legal status of the euro; the confirmation of the 1 to 1 conversion between the ECU and euro; and adoption of the Stability Pact which sets limits on any divergences between the budgetary policies conducted by future EMU Member States.

### When did the change-over to EMU take place?

The Treaty on European Union envisages two possible dates:

● 1st January 1997, if a majority of countries fulfilled the convergence criteria (as decided by the Council, based on reports by the European Commission (EC) and the EMI - Art. 109 J §3).
● 1st January 1999, for countries that fulfilled the convergence criteria (Art. 109 J §4). The Protocol on movement to the third state of EMU specifies: "If by the end of 1997, the date for the

*"The decision to go ahead with monetary union has been inspired more by the political objective of European unification than by an analysis of the costs and benefits of EMU"*

**Paul de Grauwe**
The Economics of
Monetary Integration,
Oxford, 1997

beginning of the third stage has not been set, the third stage shall start on 1st January 1999".

On this date, countries fulfilling the convergence criteria would automatically participate in EMU, excepting those which had negotiated an exemption clause. There was no minimum number of countries.

As economic convergence remained inadequate in 1997, the change-over to the single currency was postponed until 1999.

**What is the calendar for the realisation of EMU and the change-over to the single currency?**

1997: This was the reference year for assessing convergence.

Early 1998: Last realignments of exchange rates, in particular of the Greek Drachma under the assumption that this currency will enter EMU before 2002.

May 1998: Start of Stage III-A. Appraisal, based on the convergence criteria, to determine which countries participate in the single currency from 1st January 1999. Fixing of cross conversion rates among participating national currencies. Nomination of the six members of the "Directoire" of the *European Central Bank* and its President, the Dutchman, Mr Willem *Duisenberg*.

From January 1st 1999: Start of Stage III-B of EMU. Establishment of the *European System of Central Banks (ESCB)* and *ECB*, definition of the accompanying system of regulation; replacement of the ECU by the euro; irrevocable fixing of conversion rates of EMU Member States' currencies with the euro; centralised monetary policy; issuing of

securities in euro and creation of a critical mass of euros.

On this date, national currencies of participating states were replaced by the euro which became a currency in its own right. The *ECB* implements its monetary policy in euro. Countries issue a range of securities that may be paid for in euro (the same possibility will exist for taxes). Banks use the euro among themselves. Citizens can open euro accounts and make euro-denominated bank payments: the euro is a *scriptural* or book-currency.

However, it is necessary to wait until 2002 for the appearance of notes and coins in euro. The introduction of euro cash should then take place rapidly (a period of no more than 6 months). During the transition period, the national notes and coins circulate alongside euros. Although the euro remains a book-currency during this time, it has *legal tender* in all EMU Member States.

From 1st January 2002: Start of Stage III-C. The euro becomes obligatory for non-cash transactions. Notes and coins in national currency start to be replaced by euros. This replacement programme, principally aimed at automatic vending machines, takes place over a period not exceeding 6 months.

The precise conditions and timing of these aspects are framed in the national change-over plans of each state. The euro also becomes a *fiduciary* currency on January 2002.

**Why do EMU Member States have to respect convergence or "Maastricht criteria"?**

In the past, international monetary upheavals have tended to be the consequence of divergent economic and fiscal policies across countries. In order for EMU to be sustainable and the single currency to be stable, participating countries must demonstrate an adequate degree of economic convergence.

Criteria are defined in Art. 109J §1 of the Maastricht Treaty: The Commission and the EMI shall report to the *Council* on the progress made in the fulfilment by the Member States of their obligations regarding the achievement of Economic and Monetary Union. These reports shall include an examination of the compatibility between each Member State's national legislation, including the statutes of its national central bank. The reports shall also examine the achievement of a high degree of sustainable convergence by reference to the fulfilment by each Member State of the following criteria:

● the achievement of a high degree of price stability close to that of, at most, the three best performing Member States;

● the sustainability of the each government's financial position by containing public expenditures;

● the observance of the normal *fluctuation margins* provided for by the exchange rate mechanism of the European Monetary System, for at least two years, without devaluing against the currency of any other Member State;

● the durability of convergence achieved by the Member State and of its participation in the exchange-rate mechanism, of the European Monetary System, being reflected in the level of long-term interest-rate levels.

Signatory countries have fixed the following levels for these criteria:

● *inflation* must be no more than 1.5 % higher than the average of the three best performing countries;

● with regard to public finances, the net *public*

*sector deficit* of central, regional and local government, including social security, must be no higher than 3% of *gross domestic product (GDP)*, and the total national debt must be no higher than 60% of *GDP*. (It is this double definition of public finances which has prompted commentators to declare that there are in fact five convergence criteria);

● for long-term interest rates, government bond yields must be no more than 2% higher than the average of the three Member States with the lowest *inflation*.

Participating States must also make their Central Bank fully independent from the political authorities.

*Illustration 6*: "Convergence criteria status".

*Illustrations 7a, 7b, 7c*: "Convergence in EU Member States' inflation, interest rates and public deficits"

*Illustration 8*: "National debt in EU Member States 1998"

### Should the convergence criteria be flexible?

In order to alleviate the social impact of restrictive public spending, there have been calls for the convergence criteria to be relaxed. This would have required an unanimous decision of the Treaty signatories and it is not a realistic option. The Treaty foresees that the *Council* may introduce a degree of flexibility into the application of the public debt criterion, without requiring a modification of the Treaty. In addition, the final decision on who qualifies to join is "based on" the criteria; it does not require their strict application. This explains why Belgium and Italy were considered to be eligible despite public debts far in excess of the 60% limit. It also explains why Greece was asked to make further efforts before being admitted.

### Why have convergence criteria: (1) a necessary harmonisation of Member States' economic policies?

After their entry into EMU, countries maintain budgetary and fiscal autonomy. This is due to the absence of European harmonisation in this area. However, history has shown that divergent economic policies between Member States of the Union lead to variations in exchange rates. In the past, states sought to offset divergent *inflation* and productivity levels by manipulating their currencies. Such adjustments are no longer possible in EMU.

Furthermore, it is necessary to avoid the situation whereby states that practise budgetary discipline are made to pay for those that adopt a casual approach. The stability of the euro depends on all EMU Member States continuing to be strictly disciplined in the management of their public finances.

These rules are not in contradiction with the principle of solidarity between Union Member States. Indeed, they draw their inspiration directly from the essential premise of the Treaty of Rome, i.e. "the harmonious development of the whole of the Community" (Art. 130 A).

### Why have convergence criteria: (2) a reform of our society?

Economic convergence is part of a reform of society. Rigorous budgetary policies mark a departure from the excesses of the welfare state policies of the past. This new approach precludes over-indebtedness at the expense of future generations. In addition, *structural adjustment* could create economic conditions conducive to steady growth. In turn, this could improve employment prospects in Europe.

This new economic policy emphasises the role of money as the common denominator in transactions. It opposes the manipulation of the euro to compensate for divergent productivity or the inefficiency of certain sectors relative to the world market. The independence of the *European Central Bank* serves as the guarantee of a non-inflationary monetary policy.

The principle of openness to international competition was adopted in response to the dangers of "*protectionism*". *Protectionism* is contrary to the equitable distribution of wealth (the Third World, for example, justly demands "trade not aid"), it reduces overall well-being, and, sooner or later, it provokes armed conflict.

*"Monetary union lays the foundations for a community characterised by solidarity and joint risk-taking, and which requires, if it is to be sustainable, the establishment of widespread ties and political integration"*

**H. Tietmeyer**
President of the Bundesbank, in the newspaper Le Monde, 15 February 1995.

The Union Member States are all signatories to the World Trade Agreement. This agreement promotes free market competition, a principle also recognised by the Treaty on European Union. In the same way, the single currency will contribute to an improved world economic situation from which Europeans stand to benefit in the long-run.

### Why have the convergence criteria been criticised?

The initial efforts to achieve convergence in Europe coincided with a deep economic recession and high unemployment. These have far-reaching social implications. The citizen has the impression, not without reason, that it is the most underprivileged who are worst hit by the present reform of society. The situation is similar to that prevailing in under-developed countries which have undergone "*structural adjustments*".

The convergence criteria have been criticised regarding:

● the levels at which the thresholds have been set. These leave some states with a lot of ground to make up;

● their application to weak (as well as strong) economies. This could result in a high social price to be paid by some countries;

● the tight deadlines imposed;

● their appropriateness at a time of deep economic crisis;

● their role once EMU has been achieved, in view of the four cornerstones of any balanced monetary policy (employment, growth, price stability, and exchange rate stability);

● the way they are computed: public accounts must adhere to the rules established by Eurostat, the statistical office of the *European Commission (EC)*. However, it is generally recognised that some countries have met the criteria through short term measures such as the postponement of public investments.

However, the underlying idea that the Union will ultimately benefit from economic convergence has only rarely been questioned. The principle relating to the stability of the future European currency was indeed requested by consumers' associations. Moreover, the convergence criteria are part of the Treaty ratified by all Member States and even Governments with

opt-out clauses have sought to respect them. The history of instability between European currencies requires that each future EMU member clearly confirms its intention to apply a policy of rigorous monetary management. Only then will it be possible to reap the benefits of the euro.

***Do all countries participate in EMU and what lies in store for those countries that did not join in 1999?***

All EU Member States have the right to participate in EMU as soon as they comply with the convergence criteria. A country can request to join at any time, and each country's fulfilment of the necessary conditions will be analysed at least every two years.

In the first place, it is necessary to distinguish the countries that have chosen not to take part automatically in EMU, even if they fulfil the convergence criteria. The UK, Denmark and Sweden have obtained the right not to participate in EMU (the "opt-out clause"). It should also be noted that Germany's participation in EMU was subject to a vote of parliament on its degree of compliance with the convergence criteria. Then there is Greece. Greece would like to take part, but its participation has been postponed because it did not adequately fulfil several criteria.

We should point out that in 1997 a large majority of countries satisfied only three of the criteria. *Inflation* and interest rates have converged to such an extent that it is difficult, when the statistics from recent years are depicted graphically, to distinguish one country from another. The only remaining question mark was over the state of their public finances. (See illustrations 7a, 7b ).

On the basis of assessments delivered by the EMI and the *European Commission (EC)* based on actual 1997 statistics, the European *Council* made a judgement on countries' fulfilment of the convergence criteria and announced on 2 May 1998 that 11 countries would participate in EMU from 1st January 1999: Austria, Belgium, Finland, France, Germany, Ireland, Italy, Luxembourg, Netherlands, Portugal, Spain. Those countries that did not fulfil the requirements to enter EMU in 1999 or that wish to postpone their decision retain the possibility of joining later.

It is not necessarily in a country's interests to accept EMU's rigorous monetary discipline if its economy is not prepared for it. The ensuing negative impact on competitiveness and employment would very quickly become unacceptable.

The exchange rate between the currencies of countries outside EMU and the euro will fluctuate within precise limits established in the context of a new EMS that will operate with the help of the *ECB*, which policy will be fixed on the basis of the recommendations made by the *Council of the Euro*.

## What is the Council of the Euro?

The *Council of the Euro* was created in December 1997 as the political counterpart of the *European Central Bank*. It is the answer to the fears that the *ECB* would abuse its independent power at the European federal level. Its composition is made of one EC representative and the Ministers for Economy and Finance of each Member State of the EMU. It is a non-decision making group acting as adviser to *ECOFIN* on the economic policies of those States. In the Union Treaty, those policies have become "a matter of common concern" (Art. 103.1.). It also prepares the Union's positions for the international meetings, such as the *International Monetary Fund (IMF)*.

## Was there a risk that EMU might not take place or might be delayed?

Financial markets and experts considered at the end of 1997 this risk was minimal. However, numerous national and European organisations, including the *EIB*, recognised that lack of popular support did pose a threat to the successful introduction of the euro. The following events were seen at the time as having the potential to derail EMU:

● a major shock in the money markets might endanger the increasing cohesion between Member States, and threaten the achievement of economic convergence;

● failure of the countries providing the driving force behind EMU to fulfil the convergence criteria in 1998;

● serious and persistent social unrest. This could arise as a reaction to the austerity measures associated with achieving the convergence criteria especially in a period of severe economic recession. It could also arise from the far-reaching changes which the European economy undergoes, even if unrelated to the single currency;

● refusal of citizens and a large proportion of businesses to adopt the euro in the transition phase (1999 - 2002); this could cause problems for the complete withdrawal of national currencies.

● delays by governments and private businesses in implementing the euro. Ideally, the euro, for example in tax payments, in invoicing and pricing, or in payment systems should be used immediately.

Today, despite international financial upheavals of a higher amplitude than envisaged at the time, the euro has proven to be so far a success.

## 2. THE SYMBOLIC IMPORTANCE OF THE EURO

### What is the symbolic value of the euro and the philosophy behind it?

The single currency is the tangible evidence, the embodiment, of the single market and of increasingly interdependent, coordinated and convergent monetary policies. The introduction of a single currency removes the current anomaly whereby there is free circulation of persons, goods and capital, but separate monetary zones continue to be maintained.

Free flowing capital resulted often in the exchange ratio of the DEM rising as the German currency was used as refuge against a dropping USD. The GBP was, on the contrary closely following the ups and downs of the USD, unstalling undue risk in the trading relationships between the United Kingdom and its main partners.

The euro brings Europeans together in a concrete way - as did, in its day, the *European Coal and Steel Community (ECSC)*. This was the first tangible expression of the process towards European economic integration. The single currency is a vital stage on the road to prosperity and, beyond this, to lasting peace in Europe. This thesis was at the basis of Robert *Mundell*'s Nobel Prize winning research.

The single currency contributes to solidarity between Europeans. In the course of its session in Rome in October 1991, the European *Council* concluded that with the realisation of the final stage of Monetary Union, "the Community will have a stable and strong single currency - the ecu (renamed euro) - as an expression of its identity and unity".

The euro is politically neutral in a Europe where national defiance has been a persistent feature. This advantage would have been forgone if a national currency had to emerge as the driving currency, dominating the others by market force alone, without any preliminary political agreement between Member States. This is where the ecu played a critical role.

*"Europe will not be built in a day, nor will it be constructed en bloc. It will be realised in concrete stages by creating solidarity among members"*
From **Robert *Schuman*'s** address at the Salon de l'Horloge, 9 May 1950.

### When was the name "euro" chosen to designate the single currency?

The Madrid European Council (15 and 16 December 1995) took the decision to give the name euro to the single currency. "The Council considers that the name of the single currency must be the same in all the official languages of the European Union, taking into account the existence of different alphabets" ... It is a complete name, not a prefix preceding the names of national currencies. In addition, the Council specified that "the specific name 'euro' will be used in place of the generic term 'ECU' employed in the Treaty to designate the European monetary unit".
(Extract from the conclusions of the Madrid Summit, 15-16 December 1995).

In the Latin language versions of the Treaty, the single currency is referred to as the "ecu", in the masculine form, meaning the unit of account as well as the currency. In the Germanic or English language versions, the term is written "ECU" referring only to its unit of account (European Currency Unit) characteristics. The Madrid Summit put an end to this ambiguity by replacing the generic terms "ecu/ECU" with "euro" when referring to the future currency. It is an authorised "interpretation" of the text, even if opinion polls showed that a majority of Europeans, including the Germans, preferred the name "ecu".

This interpretation of the Treaty, agreed to by all 15 Heads of State or Government, removed the ambiguity which the use of the term ecu could have given. It also underlined the radical difference between the ecu-basket and a distinct European currency.

*"The single currency will symbolise in Europe the feeling of belonging to the same Community"*
**Giacobbi** et **Gronier**, "Monnaie, monnaies", Le Monde Poche No. 8610

### Will the euro entail a loss of national sovereignty?

Currency is generally perceived as a symbol of national sovereignty. If a country abandons its national currency and replaces it by a currency shared with other nations, it inevitably transfers part of that national sovereignty to a common authority. A degree of discretionary national sovereignty - notably public sector intervention - is therefore lost. The countries taking part in EMU have agreed to coordinate their economic, monetary and social policies. This reduces the power of their national parliaments and politicians in these matters.

At first, a Dane or Portuguese will feel less "at home" in his own country with the euro than with his crowns or escudos. Likewise, it can be supposed that natives of Bavaria, Savoy or Scotland, for example, felt partly deprived of their identity when national currency replaced their local currency.

Today, this is no longer a matter of concern to them. And soon, when Europeans travel abroad, they will feel more at home with the euro than when they use the dollar.

National sovereignty in monetary affairs is an illusion, particularly once countries belong to a

single commercial and financial market. The USD, the DEM, the JPY and the GBP, backed up by efficient financial markets, are the most traded currencies in international exchanges. Thus, if German interest rates were changed at the Bundesbank Council meeting, it was often the case that other central national banks followed suit. However, the Bundesbank made its decisions based on what is best for Germany, not for its neighbour countries. Secondary currencies therefore had to adapt to the dominant currencies. Indeed, the economist R. *Triffin* argued that the monetary upheavals throughout the twentieth century are largely attributable to the use of national currencies as international currency.

*"Though an indispensable requirement for the functioning of an extensive order of co-operation of free people, money has almost from its first appearance been so shamelessly abused by Governments, that it has become the prime source of disturbances of all self-ordering processes in the extended order of human co-operation"*
From **F.A. Hayek**, "The Fatal Conceit. The errors of socialism", E. Bartley 1988 p.102-103

The statutes of the *European System of Central Banks (ESCB)* and the *ECB* permit each EMU Member State to take part, in a democratic fashion, in the major monetary policy decisions regarding the euro. Furthermore, the governors of central banks of those EU Member States whose currencies are not in the first wave to be replaced by the euro, will participate as observers at relevant meetings of the *ESCB* and of the *Economic and Financial Committee (EFC)*.

The international prestige of the euro will also assist Member State citizens to affirm their European national and regional identities on the world stage.

*Will the single currency diminish our cultural identity?*

Cultural identity comprises several components: regional, national, European and international. The regional and European components will certainly be reinforced by more pronounced European integration. The single currency will support and enhance the position of Europe and its culture in the world. In making foreign travel easier, the euro will promote the reciprocal discovery of regions and countries by all Europeans. History shows that culture develops in parallel with economic strength. By strengthening the European economy, the euro will reinforce not only European culture, but also its national and regional components.

## 3. SOME CONCRETE RESULTS

*What are the advantages of the euro for businesses?*

Businesses are, as a group, the principal beneficiaries of the euro. Recent history in Europe has shown that national monetary policies cannot necessarily solve persistent economic imbalances nor prevent the over or under-valuations of currencies which, if persistent, can cause various problems for the business world.

In a market where goods and capital flow freely, businesses situated in countries with an overvalued currency see their competitiveness progressively eroded. By contrast, businesses located where currencies are correctly valued or under-valued gain in competitiveness. Prolonged overvaluation can result from too tight a monetary policy (eg. to reduce *inflation*) which involves high real interest rates. Thus businesses suffer from an uncompetitive exchange rate but also from the high interest rates which underpin the overvaluation. These high interest rates may in turn lead to recession.

A currency can be traditionally "weak", eg. the GBP and ITL, yet also be overvalued. For example, if British *inflation* is 3% and German inflation 1%, then the *GBP* must depreciate against the DEM by 2% to maintain competitiveness. If it does not, and this situation continues over many years, the GBP can become grossly overvalued against the DEM. It, however, fundamentally remains a "weak" currency while the DEM remains strong. While banks can protect businesses from short term exchange variations, they cannot do so as easily for these more fundamental exchange rate misalignments.

What all this signifies is that different national, economic and monetary policies within the Community can give rise to different *inflation* rates and levels of activity. These distortions mean there is no single market in a real sense. A single market needs a single currency and coherent economic policies. The introduction of a stable euro is likely to be accompanied by lower interest rates and economic recovery. Although there might be increased competition, businesses benefit from much simpler treasury management, price transparency, access to a euro capital market and, with the international prestige of the euro, they are able to price their exports and imports in euro instead of in USD or in JPY.

Large businesses transferring significant sums (1 million ecus) also benefit from the *Trans-European Automated Real-time Gross Settlement Transfer (TARGET)* system, one of the most modern in the world. Transfers are effected in real time. The amount appears on the recipient's account at exactly the same time it is debited from the payee's account. The *EBA clearing* system is being modernised and its

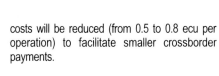

costs will be reduced (from 0.5 to 0.8 ecu per operation) to facilitate smaller crossborder payments.

While there is more competition, there will also be more opportunities for dynamic and well-prepared businesses. Above all, there will be more control over the currency fluctuations that are the main cause of distortions.

### Is the euro compatible with asymmetric shocks?

*Asymmetric shocks* occur when a key region or sector in an economy is severely confronted by some positive or negative uncontrollable event that affect it much more than the aggregate economy. For example, if oil prices were to suddenly drop significantly, Scotland and the UK would suffer social problems more severely than other EU countries. A country disposing of a national currency can use the exchange rate as one of the tools to help alleviate the difficulties and smooth the path of adjustment.

Once a country has adopted the euro, the exchange rate is no longer available to cope with an *asymmetric shock*. To cover such cases, labour will need to show more mobility than in the past and the European authorities will need to be equipped with appropriate means. This, in turn, supposes greater cross-border solidarity amongst European citizens than in the past.

### What will be the advantages of the euro for banks?

Banks will bear the heaviest part of the costs arising from the introduction of the single currency. They have to invest to adapt to the new currency and adopt international numbering of accounts to facilitate crossborder payments. They also lose a portion of their profit derived from exchanging and trading numerous currencies. The protection accorded to domestic

banks by their central banks disappears to make way for increased competition.

At first, these losses are only partially compensated for by the development of the euro and an enlargement of the European capital market. The banks also have to adopt twin-accounting systems during the transition phase in order to meet the needs of clients who wish to maintain accounts in euro and in national currency (see part 4 in this chapter). This represents a big change in countries where citizens are used to holding only one account in national currency.

### Under EMU, who controls the banks?

The Treaty on European Union (Art. 105.5) anticipates that banks remain under the control of national central banks. This situation is compatible with European regulations which impose national systems of protection for depositors. However the Treaty does not exclude conferring specific tasks upon the ECB concerning policies relating to the prudential supervision of credit institutions (Art. 105.6, together with Art. 25.2 of the ESCB/ECB statute).

### What are the advantages of the euro for the individual?

● The lives of European tourists and frontier residents is greatly simplified. When they travel they no longer have to hold several currencies to make their purchases. They are able to use automatic cash dispensers abroad with as much ease as at home. There are savings in exchange commissions for all consumers within EMU. As for commissions on crossborder payments, savings depend on the *clearing* system put in place by the *ESCB*, by national central banks and commercial banks (see the question dealing with this point in part 5.

● It is easier to compare prices in different

countries. The individual no longer mistakenly thinks that a product is expensive or cheap because he does not know the exact value of a foreign currency.

*Illustration 5*: "Price, in different EU Member States, for a Coca-Cola bottle"

● The price of goods imported from other European countries are more stable.

> *"There is nothing comparable, not even the Treaty of Rome, nor the Single Market. This is quite different from everything that has happened before, in that it will have directly noticeable effects on every single citizen"*

**Klaus *Hänsch***, former President of the *European Parliament*

Of course, all this demands a period of adaptation which, at the outset, may involve more draw-backs than advantages. This is especially true for the elderly and house-bound people. Moreover, consumers have to be on their guard, particularly at the beginning, against possible errors or abuses by tradespeople, who may try to profit as they convert local currencies into euro. This is illegal.

### What are the advantages of the single currency for the economy?

● Lower cost of capital. Real interest rates are already historically low as a result of budgetary restrictions introduced to satisfy the convergence criteria and to prepare for the single currency. Low interest rates are a key factor in bringing about a lasting improvement in Europe's economic environment.

● Disappearance of uncertainties linked to exchange risks are bound to favour investment, growth and, indirectly, employment.

● Transfer of resources to disadvantaged

areas which, like businesses, have direct access to the European capital market. *Balance of payments* deficits between countries in the euro zone do not exist.

● Money supply at the Community, rather than the national, level: a capital market on a European scale is created.

● More disciplined economic management by Member States. They are no longer able to repay their creditors in currency depreciated by *inflation*. They lose the privilege of printing banknotes to repay their debts (Art. 104 §1 of the Treaty on European Union).

● Disappearance of "competitive devaluations" within the euro zone. The single currency means that individual countries are no longer able to use devaluation to prop up their commercial competitiveness. Similarly, they are prevented from raising their interest rates - thereby generating currency over-valuation - to attract foreign capital.

● Optimisation of the advantages of the single market by eliminating one of the last remaining barriers to the free circulation of persons and goods.

### What is the international potential of the euro?

● With the USD and the JPY, the euro becomes one of the three major international currencies. This permits a more accurate reflection of the current world economic and trade situation and provides Europe with a currency in keeping with its stature as one of the largest partner in world trade.

● The negotiating power of European businesses to settle their transactions in their own currency is boosted.

● The European bond market is potentially the largest in the world. The euro is able to compete with the USD in the area of financial products. At present, around 60% of world assets are in dollars, a proportion that greatly exceeds the economic weight of the United States.

● Progressively, the euro could well become a key element in world reserves (it took more than 20 years for the USD to replace the GBP as **the** international reserve currency).

### What are the risks that EMU might fail?

● *Asymmetric shocks* (affecting one or more countries but not all), too severe to be absorbed by labour mobility, could have disastrous social consequences or force the *ECB* to bail out the country in question. This could be to the detriment of the euro's stability in international markets.

● A monetary policy which failed to maintain a balance between the four corner-stones of a sustainable monetary policy (employment, growth, price stability and exchange rate stability) could weaken the euro and trigger a rise in interest rates. In turn, this could lead to an over-valuation of the euro and increased unemployment, culminating in a political rejection of EMU. It will therefore be important to avoid a decision making process centred on the views of a single country. It is essential that all partner states' opinions are fully taken into account.

> *"...The problem is not to coordinate the pursuit of competitive deflationary measures, but to cooperate in putting in place development policies based on solidarity"*
> **Philippe Herzog**
> Le Monde, 15 September 1997

● Likewise, intense competition and the enlargement of the trading zone to the whole continent could marginalise the most vulnerable sections of the population. Pockets of poverty could take root in the most isolated regions or zones, especially those where the administrations are the least well prepared.

● Banks, weakened by the high costs of transition, and by the loss of traditional revenue from exchange commission, might no longer be able to withstand the effects of exacerbated competition. This might come from non-EU banks who are better geared to a continent-wide market and less dependent on protection at the national level.

● In the absence of a federal political authority in Europe, the monetary objectives of a federal and independent central bank might exert too great an influence over the aspirations of the individual. The economist Amartya *Sen*, Nobel Prize winner in 1998, called for a greater popular consensus on the social implications of the launching of the euro. In the words of Prof. R. *Cobbaut*: "The logic of the financial operator would dominate that of the entrepreneur" and "the consequences for society would be the alienation of the financial economy from the real one". The salutary independence of the European monetary authorities should not become overbearing.

● Europeans share a common cultural legacy. This includes democracy, with its free, pluralist and regular elections, a profound aspiration for fundamental liberties, and a just society in which privileges are matched to obligations. Will this be undermined by bringing together citizens who, in addition to these qualities, are also imbued with a sense of their own history? Cultural diversity can play a positive role in a union with others. Part of the German Münzverein's success was attributable to the capacity of federal Germany to develop the synergies between states with diverse cultures. Even so, a communal spirit and a sense of belonging were required to support a

common currency. If this paragraph has been included under the risks, and not the opportunities, which the euro represents, it is because opinion polls show that only a minority of Europeans accord European citizenship a higher priority than national citizenship. Jean *Monnet* was in the habit of saying that if Europe were to be remade from scratch, he would start with the cultural rather than the economic aspects.

*Illustration 9*: "European and national identity"

*Illustration 10*: "A European currency: for or against?"

Will the single currency succeed in welding the economically open, industrious, urbanised, modern, materialistic and dominant North to a South which, according to Luis Racionero in "El Mediterráneo y los bárbaros del Norte" (Plaza & Janes, 1985), is poorer, rural and protectionist, where aesthetics, social cohesion and "the art of living" prevail? Will anglo-saxon pragmatism be able to co-exist with the more planned and structured approach of the continental?

Cultural aspects will play a decisive role in the success of the single currency. To form a monetary union without having achieved political union is proof of pragmatism. But to hope to maintain a monetary union without political union is rash. Thus, the durability of EMU will also depend on progress in political and social integration. The limited results of the Treaty of Amsterdam (June 1997) do not augur well. An important aspect will be the capacity of EMU members to put in place new and truly European ways of management by the European institutions. The latter must be in a position to rise above the mosaic of national interests that all too often reduce them to compromises based on the lowest common denominator. The strength of the euro depends more on the joint commitment of EMU members than on their individual power.

## How does the single currency contribute to the stability of the international monetary system?

The disappearance of currencies that have regularly been subject to competitive devaluations contributes to this stability.

The priority accorded by the Treaty on European Union to stability of the euro assures it of a key role in maintaining the stability of the international monetary system (see part 6).

> *"One cannot conceive of a lasting reform of the international monetary system if Europe maintains its 11 (at that time) separate currencies"*
> **Alain Prate**, "Perspectives de l'Europe financière et monétaire", Revue Banques No. 487, October 1988

## Is the single currency not detrimental to employment?

Merely replacing national currencies does not in itself stimulate economic activity, and the simple advent of the euro does not create jobs. The disappearance of exchange transactions between EMU Member States, and increased competition between banks deprived of the privileges formerly accorded them by their national central banks, leads to job losses at an early stage. Further, the single currency does not eliminate the structural rigidities that affect the labour market. These are a major cause of high and persistent structural unemployment in many countries of the European continent.

By contrast, the elimination of exchange fluctuations (when all national currencies have been replaced by the euro) and the greater stability of the euro (included as a basic principle in the Treaty on European

Union) stimulate a recovery in European economic activity and job creation. Sustained economic growth is synonymous with increased employment.

Thanks to the Stability Pact, adopted in Dublin in December 1996, budgetary discipline will be maintained. This leads to reduced taxes and makes European labour costs more competitive, encouraging those in the "black economy" to regularise their activities.

Finally, the period of uncertainty undergone by the Community since 1990 comes to an end. A period in which Europeans develop an awareness of their potential would begin.

However, this favourable outlook is dependent on the economic policy followed by Member States, on the support they receive from the independent *ECB* and, of course, on the world outlook. The policy they adopt needs to be innovative and adapted to the new dimensions of the European monetary zone. Monetary Union is an essential element, but by itself does not bring about new employment opportunities.

*"In public debate, the importance for the economic development of the European single market around a stable currency behaviour, including a single currency, is greatly underestimated. If we succeeded in making reasonable progress in this regard, an increase in trade, with significant growth and employment gains, could be expected".*
**Michael Geuenich**, German Trades Union Federation

### Will the euro be a strong currency?

To answer this question, it is necessary to define a "strong" currency; "strong" in relation to what? How does this differ from a "stable" currency?

A "strong" currency is a currency that appreciates in value relative to others. It attracts savings and foreign capital despite offering low interest rates. It is normally accompanied by price stability (low *inflation*). It conserves its purchasing power in its home territory and is therefore considered to benefit from "internal stability".

The strength of a currency depends on the economic importance of the country it represents and the stability of its political authorities. This includes the confidence that they inspire, the degree of monetary discipline that they demonstrate and the level of cooperation among various sectors of the economy (private and public, workers and management) that they achieve.

The might of a unified European economy with a disciplined monetary policy will make the euro stronger than all national European currencies taken separately. Nevertheless, uncertainty concerning political cohesion between Member States in the absence of a federal European government, and the as yet unproven economic management of the *ECB*, leave room for lingering doubt.

A "strong" currency has many advantages: it benefits from lower interest rates and it brings down the price of imports and foreign travel. However, it also has disadvantages: it undermines the competitiveness of its businesses compared to those operating in countries with "weak" currencies that are said to practice "competitive devaluation". In summary, there can be no "strong" currency without "weak" currencies and both characterise an unstable monetary system.

Instead, one should seek to have externally "stable" currencies. This presupposes a set of internally "stable" currencies: i.e. a low *inflation* rate that maintains their intrinsic value. Hence, the importance of key convergence criterion among members of a Monetary Union.

Note that the Treaty on European Union requires not that the euro be "strong" but that it be "stable" in the framework of an open market economy with free competition (Art. 3A.2). This supposes both an internally and externally stable euro compared to the other key international currencies: the USD and the JPY. Remember that the first two European units of account were set to equal the USD. In other words, it would be contrary to European interests to have a "strong" euro, if it meant that the euro would be an "anti-dollar" currency.

While the *European Central Bank* will be responsible for maintaining the internal stability of the euro, the *Council of Economic and Finance Ministers (ECOFIN)* will be responsible for setting the theoretical exchange rate of the euro. Whether a stable international monetary system can be achieved without a formal agreement such as *Bretton Woods* remains to be seen.

In summary, to be stable in the long-term, the strength of the euro must reflect that of the European economy relative to its principal competitors in the world market. But it is the level of education, capacity for work, ingenuity, and sense of solidarity of the European people which determine their productivity and drive their economy. Thus, it is they who will determine the "strength" of their common currency. In a democracy, one has the currency one deserves.

*"Currency...is also...the most powerful instrument of economic policy, which determines in large measure all economic and social evolution. And, in this role, currency, like the language of Aesop, can be the best or the worst of things"*
**F. *Bilger***, "The Maastricht criteria: are they realistic?" (1995)

## 4. THE CHANGE-OVER FROM NATIONAL CURRENCIES TO EURO

*How did the transition from ecu to euro take place?*

On 2 May 1998, the Heads of State and Government of the European Union announced, on the basis of the recommendations of the *European Commission (EC)* and the European Monetary Institute (EMI), the countries that participate in the Economic and Monetary Union (EMU) from 1st January 1999. This decision was first discussed in the *European Parliament*. Also on that date, they set the bilateral rates of exchange of the participating currencies. They were in line with the decisions taken in Luxembourg on 12 September 1997 by the *Council of Economic and Finance Ministers (ECOFIN)*. They were aimed at freezing the cross-exchange rates between currencies participating in EMU, and reduced the risk of exchange rate turmoil during the delicate period leading up to their conversion into euro on 1st January 1999.

On 1st January 1999, the official ECU was replaced by the euro at the rate of 1 to 1. The euro became an accounting (or book) currency as the ecu before, but it is a currency "in its own right" with *legal tender* in all participating Member States, and with its own central bank. Everyone can have a euro bank account.

Also on 1st January 1999, *parities* between national currencies of EMU members and the euro were "irrevocably" fixed for each participating country (see Illustration 14b). After this date, public debt is issued in, and stock exchanges switch to, the euro. Whilst the euro cannot be imposed, no one can be prevented from using it (the "neither obligation nor prohibition" principle). Banks and business operate some form of twin-accounting system and double pricing (or triple, if one includes pricing according to weight). Euro notes and coins, however, are introduced only after sufficient time has elapsed to allow a large stock to be built up. Their introduction takes place on 1st January 2002 at the latest in EMU member countries.

In these countries holders of notes and coins in national currency then have to exchange them, free of charge, for notes and coins in euro. Bank accounts are converted into euro at the same exchange rates, as are pensions and salaries, etc. Assets and liabilities denominated in national currency will be converted into euro, without affecting the other contractual clauses, notably the rate of interest.

> *"Over a maximum period of 12 months after the decision to launch Monetary Union, all the preparations will have to be concluded for the change-over to Monetary Union itself on 1st January 1999 at the latest..... On 1st January 1999, the Union will have a distinct European currency for participating states with a single monetary policy conducted in European currency. As national currencies will still be used by the retail trade, banks will install systems to permit them to combine access to financial markets in European currency with accounts in national currency for their clients."*
> **Jacques Santer**, former President of the European Commission, 1997

By June 2002 at the latest, the euro is the sole *means of payment* with *legal tender*. National currencies of participating countries have totally disappeared. The exact change-over scenarios and the costs implied have been framed in national change-over plans. These tend to facilitate the use of the euro by citizens as from 1st January 1999 if they so desire.

### Will the single currency and national currencies circulate in parallel?

For technical reasons, the minting of a sufficient stock of cash requires considerable time. Consequently, euro notes and coins will not be available until 2002. Between January and at the latest June 2002, euros and national currencies circulate in parallel. The *parities* between the euro and the currencies being definitively fixed, it is immaterial whether one or the other is held, just as now it is immaterial whether one holds one 1 pound coin or five 20 pence coins.

### What happens to the currencies which do not participate at the start?

The Treaty on European Union envisages that countries unable to participate in EMU at its inception could later request a re-examination of their situation or automatically be the subject of a review every two years (Art. 109 K.2 of the Treaty). With the expectation that all the currencies of Union Member States will eventually enter EMU, the Treaty refers to countries not taking part in 1999 as "Member States with a derogation" and, more recently, as the "pre-ins".

The geographic zone covered by the euro can be extended as countries fulfil the convergence criteria, and as long as their entry into EMU does not lead to excessive social problems arising either in the Union or in the individual country.

The *Council* has approved, at Amsterdam in June 1997, the establishment of a new European Monetary System mark 2 on 1st January 1999. The future system is anchored to the single currency and currencies that remain outside are allowed a wide fluctuation margin (there is a consensus for it to be +/-15% in relation to *central rates*). The participation of the "pre-ins" in such a system is voluntary, and a "pre-in" is able to sign a bilateral agreement with the *ECB* undertaking to keep the fluctuation of its currency within a narrower band.

### What is the cost of transition to the single currency and who bears the cost?

The cost of transition to the euro is difficult to calculate. Citizens, businesses and, above all, banks have to make a considerable effort during this period. Estimates vary significantly according to the methods used, the figures presented by banks vary by a factor of 1 to 70. The estimates provided are difficult to interpret: some include costs arising from other events taking place at the same time such as adapting computers to overcome the millennium problem, as well as losses in earnings through the elimination of exchange commissions.

The *European Commission (EC)* has proposed that all obligatory conversions from national currency into the euro should be free of charge for citizens and tax deductible for businesses, while conversions specifically requested should be priced at cost.

It is equally important to consider the benefits which the European citizen derives from the single currency. In other words, it is necessary to compare the cost of transition to the euro with the cost, difficult to calculate but very significant, of the absence of the single currency.

The efforts required during the transition period i.e. the costs involved, are less painful if plans are made well in advance and people are helped to become familiar with the new systems. This is particularly the case for the elderly and people with impaired sight, who need more time to get used to the new notes and coins.

## 5. SOME PRACTICAL IMPLICATIONS

### What becomes of current contracts denominated in ecu or in national currency (continuity of contracts)?

Values expressed in ecu or in national currency of EMU Members States are converted into the single currency at the rates retained for transition to stage III of EMU. The interest rates linked to financial contracts such as mortgages remain unaltered, as do other contractual clauses. Changing the denomination of the currency does not entail any other modification to the contract, unless by covenant between the contracting parties.

The agreement on the legal status of the euro thus establishes the principle of the continuity of contracts, the term "contract" encompassing written, oral and implied contracts.

### Are our monetary assets not depreciating in value?

A change in the monetary unit is not synonymous with *inflation* nor does it pose a risk to the saver, investor or pensioner. Indeed, the change affects both assets and liabilities equally. Monetary Union is not another *monetary reform*. Financial assets, like credits, are simply converted into euro at the same rates as the prices of goods. Of course, the nominal values of bonds and securities continue to vary according to market forces, but in euro, instead of in the national currencies in which they were originally issued.

Furthermore, the single currency is managed within a rigorous institutional framework aimed at price stability which in turn brings about stability in purchasing power. The independence of the *ESCB* is a guarantee that it will adhere to its mission and protects the euro from inflationary pressures. Finally, only sufficiently convergent countries participate in EMU.

### Ecu transaction costs were high. What happens with the euro?

Exchange commissions amounted annually to around 20 billion ecu. This constituted an impediment to the efficient functioning of the European economy. The amount represented 0.5% of EU countries' *GDP*. (Source EU Information, August 1995).

With the euro, transferring money within the euro-zone is less expensive, since exchange transactions are no longer necessary. However, transfers abroad could, for a time at least, remain more onerous than domestic transfers since exchange commission is not the only cost element. These costs depend more particularly on the *clearing* systems put in place: *TARGET*, *EBA*, or systems established with bank groups.

### At what rates are national currencies converted into euro?

From 1999, national currencies of EMU Member States and the euro are merely different subdivisions of the same currency, the euro. There is no longer any exchange in the sense that no further alteration to conversion rates is possible. This is why one speaks of "conversion" and not "exchange" rates. As there is no risk, the buying and selling rates of the euro are identical. Banks convert their national currency into euro and vice-versa without risk.

The rates at which national currencies are converted into euro are known since 1st January 1999. Member States fixed their conversion rates to the euro by unanimous decision. Since 31st December 1998, official conversion rates from the eleven currencies participating in EMU have come into force. Consequently and since 1st January 1999, the ECU has definitely been replaced by the euro.

The legal framework of the euro provided that

conversion had to take place with 6 significant figures (decimals = 6 - number of units); for example: 1 euro = 40,3399 LUF giving 4 (6 - 2) decimals or GBP 0,711100 giving 6 (6 - 0) decimals. This is to avoid "rounding" to the advantage of one of the contracting parties.

Further, every conversion has to be from the euro towards the national currency and not the reverse i.e. 1 euro = x national currency units and not 1 national currency unit = y euros. Every exchange between two national currencies has to be via the official conversion rates with the euro. In practice, details of the procedure may vary slightly upon condition that the procedure remains verifyable.

### How to round the converted amounts into euro?

These questions are answered in articles 4 and 5 of regulation no. 1103/97 of the *Council* of 17 June 1997. They will be applicable in EMU Member States only up to 30 June 2002, at the latest, when national currencies will disappear.

First of all, it is absolutely necessary a) to start from the official conversion rate given by the counter-value of 1 euro; b) the resulting amount cannot be rounded to less than 3 decimals and is then c) converted again into the second national currency. No other calculation method is allowed unless it produces the same results.

Example: Conversion of GBP 7- in ITL;
         or GBP 7- in FRF
a) conversion GBP in EUR :
    GBP 7- /0.711100 = EUR 9.843903
    ==> b) EUR 9.844 (rounding)
c) conversion EUR in ITL:
    EUR 9.844* 1936.27 = ITL 187632.958-
    ==> d) ITL 187633- (rounding, ITL having no subdivision)
c) conversion EUR in FRF:
    EUR 9.844* 6.5596 = FRF 64.5727-
    ==> d) FRF 64.57 (rounding)

After conversion into a national monetary unit, the amounts to be paid or accounted are rounded to the nearest next or preceding subdivision. If, once applied, the conversion rate gives a result that falls exactly in the middle, the amount is rounded to the next figure upward.

As an example: a final conversion, giving 34.874 will be rounded to 34.87 euros. If the conversion produces 34.876, the final result will be 34.88 euros. A conversion giving 34.8750 will be rounded to 34.88.

*Illustration 11*: "From ecu to euro"

*Illustration 12*: "Notes in euro"

*Illustration 13*: "Coins in euro"

*Illustration 14a*: "Euro Conversion and Exchange rates

*Illustration 14b*: "Bilateral conversion rates between currencies participating in the EMU applicable from 01.01.1999"

## 6. THE EURO AFTER ITS LAUNCH

### How has the euro performed on the financial markets?

In several respects, the euro has exceeded expectations. The switch to euros for bank and stockmarket operations proceeded very smoothly and 6 months on, the volume of euro transactions on capital markets has outstripped that of dollar transactions. By June 1999 the euro was held to be a great success on the bond markets: bonds worth over EUR 270 billions had been issued on international markets in the first 6 months of 1999, compared with EUR 155 billions in the currencies which now make up the euro in the same period in 1998. Furthermore, access to this market has become easier for companies: by June 1999, corporates had issued a total of

EUR 70 billions on the euro market, compared with EUR 20 billions over the same period in 1998. Lastly, local and regional authorities, which in the past had to pass through national authorities to access the international capital markets can now secure direct funding on the international euro market. Stockmarkets have also recognised the euro as a reference currency in Europe since stocks are now priced in euro in all stock markets of euroland. Several European stockmarket indices have been created.

### Has the increased transparency brought about by the euro affected consumer prices?

Since the euro was introduced there has been a - downward - convergence of the prices of certain products, for example cars, from which the consumer is now benefiting. There have also been alignments in the tourism sector, particularly as regards transport costs. The trend would certainly have been more marked had there been greater tax harmonisation, called for also by companies aware of the fact that tax differentials make price differences more obvious to the consumer. Value added tax on cars for instance still vary from  15 % in Luxembourg to 22 % in Finland (25 % in Denmark and Sweden). Inflation has remained very low (less than 2% per annum) due to a tight fiscal policy and the independence of the *European Central Bank*, which has continued to apply the Treaty on European Union to the better.  The greater competition within the single market has also contributed to this positive development. However, at consumer level, prices are still labelled mainly in national currencies. Based on the trend over the first 6 months, however, one can expect that the euro will greatly improve price transparency in the years to come.

### How has the euro evolved on the exchange markets?

The euro had a disappointing start on the foreign exchange markets. Launched on the assumption that it would be a "strong" currency, it fell during its first 6 months against the USD the international benchmark currency. At one time it even lost as much as 16% against its value on 1st January 1999, rallying slightly thereafter. However this trend is not disturbing. The international financial system is one of floating exchange rates . They are the result of financial (interest rate variations), economic (growth) and political (confidence in political authorities responsible for currency management) factors. Euro interest rates have remained low because inflation was limited and because of the poor economic performance of euro-zone countries. As far as politics is concerned, Europe-wide political power is still virtually non-existent (see below). So, a weakening of the euro was in the making.

It is also worth noting that the changes in the euro/dollar exchange rate have followed more or less the same pattern as the euro's predecessor, the ECU, and that it has not fallen in value as much as the major EMU currencies would probably have. It should also be remembered that the euro replaced the ECU on a 1 to 1 parity, the ECU having replaced previous European units of account whose rates had been set at 1 to 1 USD (see chapter 1). Hence, a "bottom line" of 1 to 1 to the USD would not be unexpected and, in the past the ECU has even fallen below that parity.

*Illustration 15*: "Historical development of the ecu and the euro against the USD"

Throughout this sensitive period, the new *European Central Bank* has demonstrated its professional expertise and through its prudence has established a degree of confidence in the euro and stability to its exchange rate . The euro is today recognised as a  stable, rather than a "strong" or "weak" currency.

### Has the euro already impacted on economic growth and employment?

Six months is too short for a new currency to

have any impact on these two elements of a sustained monetary policy.

Although an overwhelming majority of companies declare billing in euro only or in dual currency, they complain that only a minority of their suppliers actually bill in euro, which is a more reliable measuring rod of the proportion of actual trade conducted in euro. In particular, small and medium companies still very much operate in national currencies. In April 1999, less than 20% of the companies were filing their accounts in euro; Finland, Luxembourg, Austria and France are the most advanced with about 30%.

One of the euro's main handicaps has been a lack of popular support - a problem the ECU had also suffered from. Only 1-2% of the population have converted their bank accounts to euros and use the euro for payments. Citizens in EMU countries at large remain unaware that the euro **is** their official currency, that banks use the euro for inter-bank payments and that bills and coins are only monetary signs of the euro. Admittedly, consumers will feel the need to use the euro only when bank notes and coins will become available. Also, bank charges for cross-border payments remain high, including in euro, making these payments less attractive and thus restricting the use of the euro in cross-border commercial transactions which should be one of its greatest comparative advantage. Such payments are certainly cheaper than using national currencies, but charges are still too high. Thus, after six months there has still been too little change in the pre-euro situation for the single currency to have had a perceptible effect on the economy and employment.

### Why are crossborder payments complicated and expensive?

Transfers across borders[2] really pose 3 sorts of problems. First, they take a lot more time to execute than national transfers. Second, they are more expensive because of a system of double charging (by the sender's bank and that of the beneficiary). Third, when funds go astray in the international banking circuit (failed transfers), their recovery by the sender is often difficult. Why these complications? Because these payments go through more than one banking network. They are often handled by several intermediary banks, and there can be a split between the international and domestic parts of the payment if there is no link between the *SWIFT* network and national systems. Some central banks also ask a fee to cover costs of keeping statistics. The problems and high costs are associated with the transfer of small amounts, unless they can be grouped.

### Will cross-border bank transfers improve?

In January 1997 the *European Parliament* adopted a directive on crossborder transfers between EMU Member States, which facilitate transfers of less than 50 000 ecus/euros and increase transparency in this regard. EMU States have to apply the directive within 30 months.

Three principles are involved. First, unless otherwise agreed by the parties, the funds must be credited to the beneficiary's account within 6 working days. Second, double charging is not allowed. Costs are borne exclusively by the sender. In addition, the costs are not payable if the transfer takes longer than 6 working days. Third, if the transfer fails, then the sender's bank has to reimburse its client, within a fortnight, the full value of the transfer (up to 12 500 euros), plus all costs.
Furthermore, central banks have to take measures to facilitate international payments. In parallel, commercial banks inaugurate their own compatible systems. Finally, all European banks are encouraged to adopt the "Identification Bank Account Number" (IBAN) to simplify international

2. Promeuro is indebted to the "Banque Populaire de Lorraine" for some of the answers to these questions.

transfers. All bank codes would then comprise two digits of country-code, a two character overall control key, followed by a local account number. This system has been adopted by the International Standard Organisation (ISO), which establishes global norms in October 1997. It is recommended by the Banking Federation of the European Union.

### How does one understand the new prices of goods?

During the run-up period, prices displayed in shops as well as wages and salaries, pensions, bank statements etc., are available in both national currency and in euro. Many companies are printing the ecu equivalent on wage and salary slips in order to familiarise employees with the amount in euro.

Simple calculators or conversion tables are being distributed by shops or banks to facilitate the conversion of the single currency into the former national currencies, and vice versa. Before becoming entirely accustomed to the euro, Europeans feel like tourists in their own countries, obliged to convert prices into their national currencies to "understand" them. After a period of adaptation, during which prices, wages, taxes, bank statements, pensions, etc., are expressed in euros, Europeans begin to "think" in euros and do no longer need to refer back to their former national currencies.

### What has been the evolution on the political front?

Integration at political level has been slow but encouraging signs have begun to appear. No agreement has been reached, for example, on a single euro-zone representation in international authorities and bodies, thus depriving the euro of one of the main benefits it ought to be bringing to Europe, namely enhanced international standing and greater confidence in the European

*"The single currency
will serve those who
prepare for it"*

**Jean Claude** *Juncker*
Prime Minister of
Luxembourg, from the
Echo news,
9 October 1995

endeavour. EMU member countries continue to present themselves in dispersed order in international gatherings, loosing hereby much of their potential clout, in relation to the world powers such as the USA and Japan. Considerable hope has been placed in the new Commission presided by Romano Prodi to renovate the European Institutions to make them more compatible with the federal system operating in monetary matters. Surveys suggest that a majority of European citizens expect a major overhaul of these institutions. The success of the euro has played a role in the growing awareness of the need to accelerate political integration. A new Intergovernmental Conference among EU members is planned.

## 7. ... AND IN 2002

### What will our wallets contain in 2002?

Seven notes in denominations of 5, 10, 20, 50, 100, 200 and 500 euros. These notes were presented to the public at the Dublin Summit in December 1996.

Eight coins in denominations of 0.01, 0.02, 0.05, 0.1, 0.2, 0.5, 1 euro and 2 euros. The sub-units of the euro are officially called "eurocent" and, in everyday language, known as "cent" (Anglo-Saxon pronunciation). This does not preclude alternative pronunciations in other languages. The term "eurocents" appears on coins to distinguish them from American cents. These coins have one side common to all countries and one side carrying a national symbol, but they have *legal tender* in all EMU member countries.

### What security measures are taken to protect against falsification of the euro?

A number of modern security systems will be incorporated into euro bank notes so that their protection against counterfeiting are at least as good as for existing notes in national currency. The judicial framework adopted in Dublin requires Member States to take all necessary measures against counterfeiting.

### Are bank notes identifiable by people with impaired sight?

The needs of the blind and partially sighted people have been taken into consideration in the technical specifications. To facilitate identification of the various euro denominations, the notes have been given clearly distinguishable sizes and colours according to their face value. Their value is clearly marked in the same place on both sides across the whole range of denominations, and also in Braille. The change-over period from national to euro notes and coins has been initially set at six months to allow the old, the blind, and those with poor sight to get accustomed, but shorter periods are envisaged by several member countries.

### Do the coins contain metals such as nickel which can provoke allergies?

Coins will be minted by national central banks. For security reasons, coins of 1 and 2 euros contain nickel. The other coins do not.

### Who needs to prepare for the single currency?

Everyone is affected by EMU in daily life and we all have to make an effort to learn and adapt. Particular demands are placed upon citizens banks and small and medium-sized businesses. Numerous adjustments are necessary, notably in the areas of accounting and information technology. Experience in January 1999 have shown that the feared period of transition has finally passed without the announced catastrophies.

# *a*ppendices

 *a*ppendix **1**

## Illustrations

Country and currency abbreviations

| Code | Country name | Code | Currency name |
|------|--------------|------|---------------|
| AT | Austria | ATS | Austrian shilling |
| BE | Belgium | BEF | Belgian franc |
| DE | Germany | DEM | German mark |
| DK | Denmark | DKK | Danish krone |
| ES | Spain | ESP | Spanish peseta |
| FI | Finland | FIM | Finnish mark |
| FR | France | FRF | French franc |
| GB | United Kingdom | GBP | Pound sterling |
| GR | Greece | GRD | Greek drachma |
| IE | Ireland | IEP | Irish pound |
| IT | Italy | ITL | Italian lira |
| LU | Luxembourg | LUF | Luxembourg franc |
| NL | Netherlands | NLG | Dutch florin |
| PT | Portugal | PTE | Portuguese escudo |
| SE | Sweden | SEK | Swedish kronor |
| EU | European Union | EUR | Euro |

# Illustration 1

Appeal by Esperanto users for a single currency in Europe

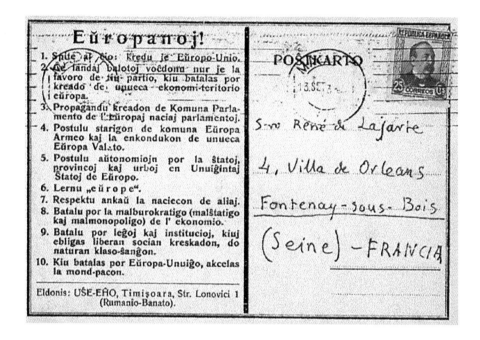

*Translated from Romanian, this reads:*

**Europeans!**

1.  In spite of everything, **affirm your belief in European union**.
2.  In national elections, vote only for parties which promote the creation of a unified European economic zone.
3.  Propagate the idea of the creation of a parliament to represent all national parliaments.
4.  **Demand** the establishment of a common European amy, as well as the
    **introduction of a single European currency**.
5.  Demand autonomy for states, provinces and towns at the heart of the United States of Europe.
6.  **Study "European"**
7.  Respect the nationality of others.
8.  Fight against increased bureaucracy (and in favour of denationalisation and demonopolisation).
9.  Fight for laws and institutions which permit free social development, thus class mobility.
10. Those who strive for the European Union assist world peace.

# Illustration 2

Composition of the ecu basket

**1 Ecu = x %
of the following
currencies:**

**in bold: currencies
of EMU countries**

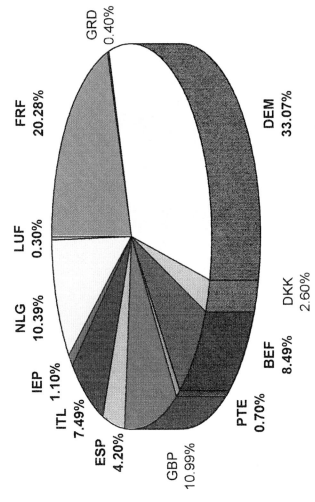

Illustration 2: Composition of the ecu basket

GRD 0.40%

FRF 20.28%

DEM 33.07%

LUF 0.30%

NLG 10.39%

IEP 1.10%

ITL 7.49%

ESP 4.20%

GBP 10.99%

PTE 0.70%

BEF 8.49%

DKK 2.60%

# Illustration 3

Evolution of the ecu delta

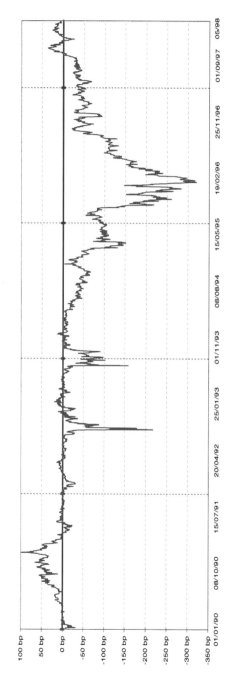

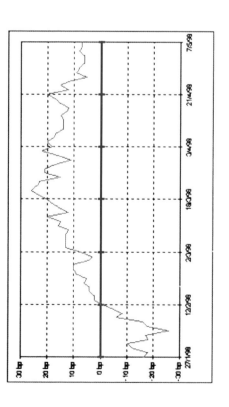

# Illustration4a

Historic value of seven EU currencies (plus USD and JPY) against the ecu/euro 1980-1999

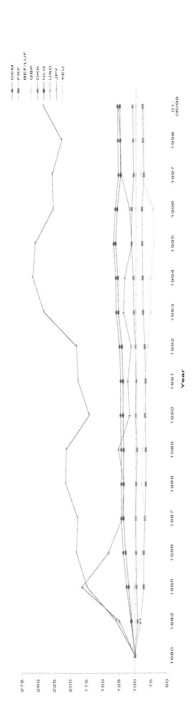

# Illustration4b

Historic value of the remaining eight EU currencies (plus USD) against the ecu/euro 1980-1999

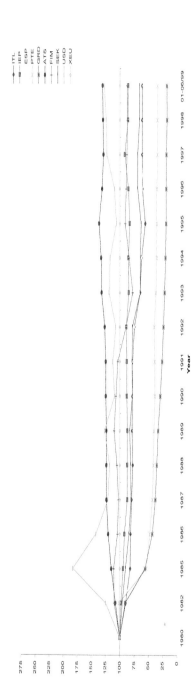

# Illustration 5

Price, in different EU Member States, for a Coca-Cola bottle

| Countries | Price | | Price in Ecus | % compared to minimum price |
|---|---|---|---|---|
| France | FRF | 6.50 | 0.98 | 128% |
| Belgium | BEF | 48.00 | 1.18 | 153% |
| Germany | DEM | 3.02 | 1.53 | 199% |
| Spain | ESP | 125.00 | 0.77 | 100% |
| Ireland | IEP | 0.93 | 1.19 | 154% |
| Italy | ITL | 2,460.00 | 1.26 | 164% |
| Luxembourg | LUF | 42.00 | 1.03 | 134% |
| Portugal | PTE | 199.00 | 0.99 | 128% |
| United-Kingdom | GBP | 1.09 | 1.63 | 212% |

Source: Bureau Européen des Unions de Consommateurs (BEUC), ECU rates 24 July 1998

# Illustration 6
Convergence criteria status

| | Inflation | | | Interest Rate | | | Public sector deficit % GDP | | | National debt % GDP | | |
|---|---|---|---|---|---|---|---|---|---|---|---|---|
| | 1997 | 1998 | Diff. | 1997 | 1998 | Diff. | 1997 | 1998 | Diff. | 1997 | 1998 | Diff. |
| Austria | 1.8 | 1.5 | -0.3 | 5.7 | 5.6 | -0.1 | 2.5 | 2.3 | -0.2 | 66.1 | 64.7 | -1.4 |
| Belgium | 1.6 | 1.3 | -0.3 | 5.8 | 5.7 | -0.1 | 2.1 | 1.7 | -0.4 | 122.2 | 118.1 | -4.1 |
| Denmark | 2.3 | 2.1 | -0.2 | 6.2 | 6.2 | 0.0 | -0.7 | -1.1 | 0.4 | 65.1 | 59.5 | -5.6 |
| Finland | 1.4 | 2.0 | 0.6 | 6.0 | 5.9 | -0.1 | 0.9 | -0.3 | -1.2 | 55.8 | 53.6 | -2.2 |
| France | 1.1 | 1.0 | -0.1 | 5.6 | 5.5 | -0.1 | 3.0 | 2.9 | -0.1 | 58.0 | 58.1 | 0.1 |
| Germany | 1.9 | 1.7 | -0.2 | 5.7 | 5.6 | -0.1 | 2.7 | 2.5 | -0.2 | 61.3 | 61.2 | -0.1 |
| Greece | 5.5 | 4.5 | -1.0 | 9.9 | 9.8 | -0.1 | 4.0 | 2.2 | -1.8 | 108.7 | 107.7 | -1.0 |
| Ireland | 1.4 | 3.3 | 1.9 | 6.3 | 6.2 | -0.1 | -0.9 | -1.1 | -0.2 | 66.3 | 59.5 | -6.8 |
| Italy | 2.4 | 2.1 | -0.3 | 6.9 | 6.7 | -0.2 | 2.7 | 2.5 | -0.2 | 121.6 | 118.1 | -3.5 |
| Luxembourg | 1.4 | 1.6 | 0.2 | 5.8 | 5.6 | -0.2 | -1.7 | -1.0 | 0.7 | 6.7 | 7.1 | 0.4 |
| Netherlands | 2.2 | 2.3 | 0.1 | 5.8 | 5.5 | -0.3 | 1.4 | 1.6 | 0.2 | 72.1 | 70.0 | -2.1 |
| Portugal | 2.1 | 2.2 | 0.1 | 6.4 | 6.2 | -0.2 | 2.5 | 2.2 | -0.3 | 62.0 | 60.0 | -2.0 |
| Spain | 2.5 | 2.2 | -0.3 | 6.4 | 6.3 | -0.1 | 2.6 | 2.2 | -0.4 | 68.8 | 67.4 | -1.4 |
| Sweden | 2.2 | 1.5 | -0.7 | 6.6 | 6.5 | -0.1 | 0.8 | -0.5 | -1.3 | 76.6 | 74.1 | -2.5 |
| United Kingdom | 2.3 | 2.3 | 0.0 | 7.0 | 7.0 | 0.0 | 1.9 | 0.6 | -1.3 | 53.4 | 52.3 | -1.1 |
| EUR-15 | 2.1 | 1.9 | | 6.3 | 6.1 | | 2.6 | 2.4 | -0.2 | 72.1 | 70.5 | -1.6 |
| NORMS | 2.7 | 2.7 | | 8.0 | 7.8 | | 3.0 | 3.0 | | 60.0 | 60.0 | |

in conformity with the criteria or improving

# Illustration 7a

Convergence in EU Member States' inflation rates

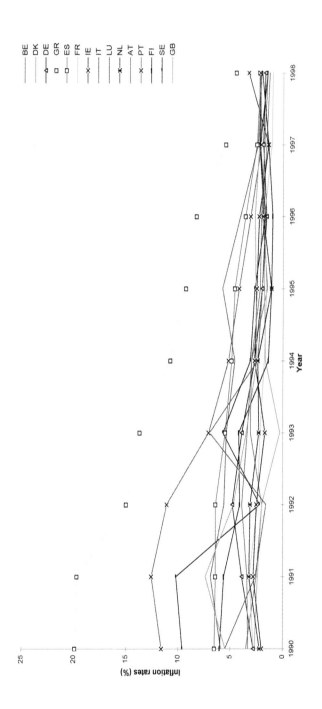

# Illustration 7b

Convergence in EU Member States' long-term nominal interest rates

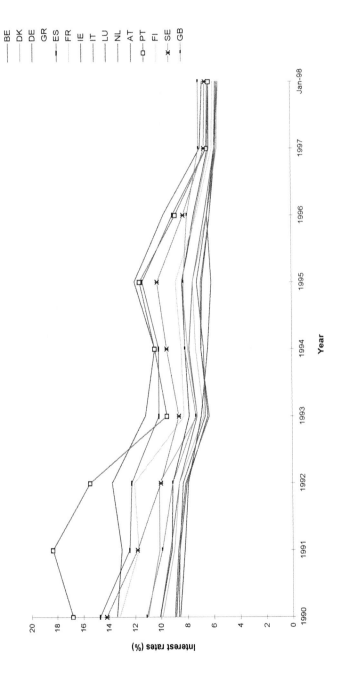

# Illustration7c

Evolution of public sector deficits

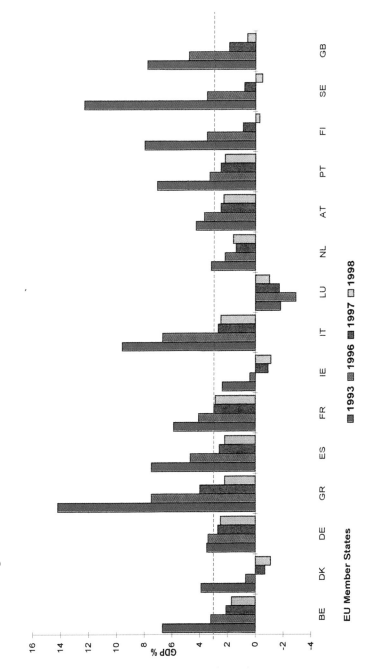

# Illustration 8

National debt in EU Member States 1998 (in ECU per inhabitant and in % of GDP)

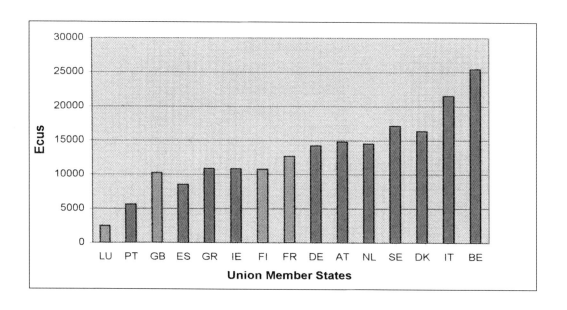

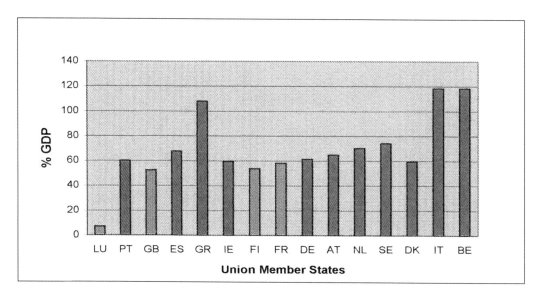

# Illustration9

## European and National identity

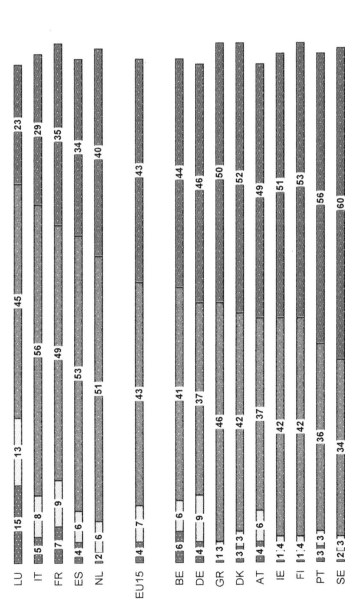

LU  15  13  45  23

IT  5  8  56  29

FR  7  9  49  35

ES  4  6  53  34

NL  2  6  51  40

EU15  4  7  43  43

BE  6  6  41  44

DE  4  9  37  46

GR  1 3  46  50

DK  3 3  42  52

AT  4  6  37  49

IE  1 4  42  51

FI  1 4  42  53

PT  3 3  36  56

SE  2 3  34  60

GB  5  4  27  62

☐ % European identity
☐ % European and national identity

☐ % National and European identity
☐ % National identity

March/April 1999

Percentage "don't know" not shown

# Illustration 10

The euro: for or against?

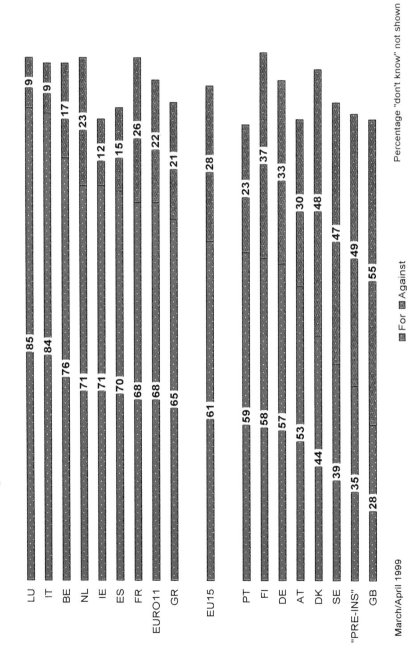

| | For | Against |
|---|---|---|
| LU | 85 | 9 |
| IT | 84 | 9 |
| BE | 76 | 17 |
| NL | 71 | 23 |
| IE | 71 | 12 |
| ES | 70 | 15 |
| FR | 68 | 26 |
| EURO11 | 68 | 22 |
| GR | 65 | 21 |
| EU15 | 61 | 28 |
| PT | 59 | 23 |
| FI | 58 | 37 |
| DE | 57 | 33 |
| AT | 53 | 30 |
| DK | 44 | 48 |
| SE | 39 | 47 |
| "PRE-INS" | 35 | 49 |
| GB | 28 | 55 |

March/April 1999

Percentage "don't know" not shown

# Illustration 11

From ecu to euro...

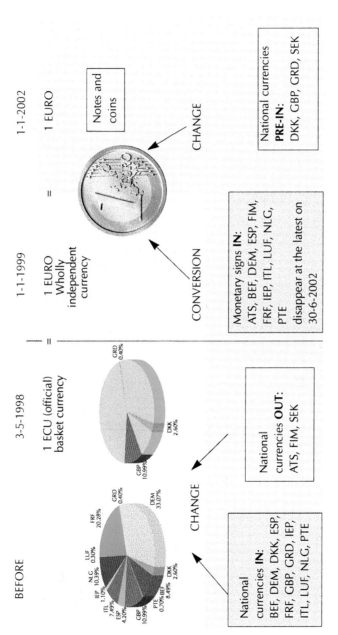

BEFORE 3-5-1998 1-1-1999 1-1-2002

1 ECU (official) basket currency

1 EURO Wholly independent currency

1 EURO

Notes and coins

CONVERSION

CHANGE

Monetary signs **IN**:
ATS, BEF, DEM, ESP, FIM, FRF, IEP, ITL, LUF, NLG, PTE
disappear at the latest on 30-6-2002

National currencies **PRE-IN**:
DKK, GBP, GRD, SEK

National currencies **OUT**:
ATS, FIM, SEK

CHANGE

National currencies **IN**:
BEF, DEM, DKK, ESP, FRF, GBP, GRD, IEP, ITL, LUF, NLG, PTE

GRD 0.40%
DKK 2.60%
GBP 10.99%

DEM 33.07%
FRF 20.28%
GRD 0.40%
LUF 0.30%
NLG 10.39%
IEP 1.10%
ITL 7.49%
ESP 4.20%
GBP 10.99%
PTE 0.70%
BEF 8.49%
DKK 2.60%

**1 ECU = 1 euro: unchanged external parity ( Art. 109.L.4 Maastricht Treaty)**

Accounting currencies

Bank notes and coins

# Illustration 12

Notes in euro

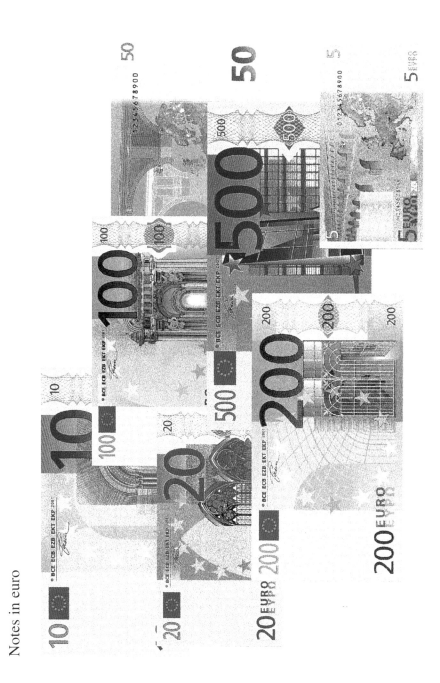

# Illustration 13

Coins in euro

# Illustration 14a

Exchange rates against the euro (as of 1 January 1999)

**Conversion rates irrevocably fixed between the Euro and the currencies of the EMU Member States (as of 1 January 1999)**

| CURRENCY - Country | | RATE 1 EURO = |
|---|---|---|
| DEM | Germany | 1.95583 |
| ATS | Austria | 13.7603 |
| BEF | Belgium | 40.3399 |
| ESP | Spain | 166.386 |
| FIM | Finland | 5.94573 |
| FRF | France | 6.55957 |
| IEP | Ireland | 0.787564 |
| ITL | Italy | 1936.27 |
| LUF | Luxembourg | 40.3399 |
| NLG | Netherlands | 2.20371 |
| PTE | Portugal | 200.482 |

**Exchange rates against the Euro (on 04/01/1999)**

| CURRENCY - COUNTRY | | RATE 1 EURO = |
|---|---|---|
| DKK | Denmark | 7.4501 |
| GBP | United Kingdom | 0.7111 |
| GRD | Greece | 327.15 |
| SEK | Sweden | 9.4696 |
| USD | United States | 1.1789 |
| JPY | Japan | 133.73 |

# Illustration 14b

Bilateral conversion rates between currencies participating in the EMU applicable from 01.01.1999

| | 100 BEF/LUF | 100 FRF | 100 DEM | 1 IEP | 100 NLG | 100 PTE | 100 ESP | 100 ATS | 100 FIM | 1000 ITL |
|---|---|---|---|---|---|---|---|---|---|---|
| Belgium/Lux. | - | 614.977 | 2062.55 | 51.2210 | 1830.55 | 20.1214 | 24.2447 | 293.162 | 678.468 | 20.8338 |
| France | 16.2608 | - | 335.386 | 8.32893 | 297.661 | 3.27189 | 3.94237 | 47.6704 | 110.324 | 3.38773 |
| Germany | 4.84837 | 29.8164 | - | 2.48338 | 88.7517 | 0.975559 | 1.17547 | 14.2136 | 32.8947 | 1.01010 |
| Ireland | 1.95232 | 12.0063 | 40.2676 | - | 35.7582 | 0.392834 | 0.473335 | 5.72347 | 13.2459 | 0.406743 |
| Netherlands | 5.46285 | 33.5953 | 112.674 | 2.79812 | - | 1.09920 | 1.32445 | 16.0150 | 37.0637 | 1.13812 |
| Portugal | 496.984 | 3056.34 | 10250.5 | 254.56 | 9097.53 | - | 120.492 | 1456.97 | 3371.88 | 103.541 |
| Spain | 412.462 | 2536.54 | 8507.22 | 211.267 | 7550.3 | 82.9929 | - | 1209.18 | 2798.42 | 85.9313 |
| Austria | 34.1108 | 209.774 | 703.552 | 17.4719 | 624.415 | 6.86357 | 8.27006 | - | 231.431 | 7.10657 |
| Finland | 14.7391 | 90.6420 | 304.001 | 7.54951 | 269.806 | 2.96571 | 3.57345 | 43.2094 | - | 3.07071 |
| Italy | 4799.90 | 29518.3 | 99000.2 | 2458.56 | 87864.4 | 965.805 | 1163.72 | 14071.5 | 32565.8 | - |

PROMEURO

# Illustration 15

Historical Development of the ecu and the euro against the USD

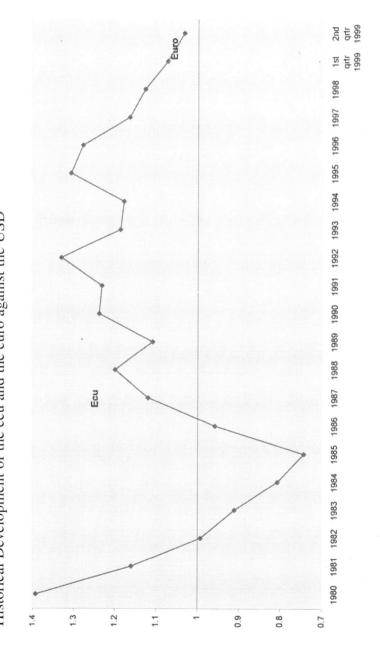

# $\mathcal{A}$ppendix $2$
# Historical development

## a. The early years (1994-1976)
Critical stages in the post-war period leading up to Economic and Monetary Union

| Year | Treaties and proposals | European Institutions | Monetary Development |
|---|---|---|---|
| 1944 | *Bretton Woods* Agreement | | USD is the international anchor currency |
| 1948 | Creation of the EOEC: *European Organisation for Economic Cooperation* | | |
| 1949 | The Hague Conference and Westminster Congress | | |
| 1950 | (9 May) *R. Schuman's* speech at the "Salon de l'Horloge" | Creation of the Europe an Payments Union (EPU) | European unit of of account (EUA) 1 EUA = 1 USD |
| 1952 | Creation of the *European Coal & Steel Community (ECSC)* | | |
| 1957/ 1958 | Treaty of Rome: creation of the European Economic Community (EEC) (Belgium, France, Italy, Luxembourg, The Netherlands, Germany) (comes into force in 1958) | European Monetary Agreement (EMA) (replaces EPU) | |
| 1962 | | The Community's first monetary expression | Unit of account (UA) 1 UA = 1 EUA |
| 1964 | | Creation of the Committee of Central Bank Governors | |
| 1970 | *Werner* Plan: first full-scale plan for establishing a Monetary Union in Europe | | |

| Year | Treaties and proposals | European Institutions | Monetary Development |
|------|------------------------|------------------------|----------------------|
| 1971 | United States relinquish USD *convertability* into gold Smithsonian Institute (Washington D.C.) Agreement | | Introduction of the "*tunnel*" for international currencies |
| 1972 | Basle Agreement | | "*Snake* (for European currencies) in the *tunnel*" |
| 1973 | First Oil Crisis. International currencies are floated. The United Kingdom, Ireland and the Denmark join the EEC | Creation of *European Monetary Cooperation Fund (EMCF)* (replaces the Board of Governors) | "*Snake* without the *tunnel*" |
| 1975 | *Fourcade* and *Tindemans* reports | | |
| 1976 | | | *Snake* limited to stable currencies |

## b. Development since the creation of the ECU (1978-1996)

| | | | |
|------|------------------------|------------------------|----------------------|
| 1978/ 1979 | Aix-la-Chapelle Summit; creation of European Monetary System (EMS) | | Creation of European Currency Unit (ECU) (official use) 1 official ECU = 1 UA |
| 1981 | SOFTE and *EIB* launch first ecu-denominated bonds Greece becomes the 10th member of the EEC | | Creation of the private ecu in capital markets 1 ecu = 1 ECU |
| 1985 | *Genscher-Colombo* Plan: the Milan Council requests that the Treaty of Rome be revised | | |
| 1986 | Spain and Portugal join the EEC | | |
| 1987 | Single Act comes into force | | |
| 1989 | *Delors* Plan: transition to the single currency via the parallel currency | | Freedom of capital movements |
| 1990 | Stage 1 of the transition to Economic and Monetary Union (EMU) | | |
| 1992 | Treaty on European Union signed at Maastricht. First referenda in Denmark & France | Single Market comes into force | |

| Year | Treaties and proposals | European Institutions | Monetary Development |
|---|---|---|---|
| 1993 | Second referendum in Denmark. Ratification of the Treaty on European Union | | |
| 1994 | Launch of Stage II of EMU | Creation of the European Monetary Institute (EMI) (replaces EMCF) | |
| 1995 | Madrid Summit: Confirmation of process leading to EMU. Austria, Finland and Sweden join the Union | | Future single currency will be called the euro |
| 1996 | Dublin Summit: the euro's legal framework established | | The euro will replace the ECU at the rate of 1 for 1 |

## c. The first steps (1997-2002)

| | | | |
|---|---|---|---|
| 1997 | Reference year for measuring compliance with convergence criteria to determine first wave of EMU Member States | | |
| 1998 | May: Stage III-A Selection of countries that will adopt the euro in 1999 | Nomination of the first President of the *European Central Bank (ECB)*: Mr Willem *Duisenberg* | Fixing of cross conversion rates between national currencies participating to EMU |
| 1999 | Stage III-B Introduction of the euro in the first wave of countries | The *European Central Bank (ECB)* replacing EMI | Irreversible fixing of euro parities. The euro becomes *scriptural money* 1 ECU = 1 euro |
| 2002 | January: Stage III-C | | National currencies progressively replaced by the euro that becomes *fiduciary money* |
| 6/2002 | June: EMU | | National currencies of first wave countries totally replaced by the euro |

# *a*ppendix 3
## Extracts from the Treaty on European Union

## General Articles

Art. 2. The Community shall have as its task, by establishing a common market and an Economic and Monetary Union and by implementing the common policies or activities referred to in Articles 3 and 3a, to promote throughout the Community a harmonious and balanced development of economic activities, sustainable and   non inflationary growth respecting the environment, a high degree of convergence of economic performance, a high level of employment and of social protection, the raising of the standard of living and quality of life, and economic and social cohesion and solidarity among Member States.

## The Economic Policy

Art. 103.1. Member States shall regard their economic policies as a matter of common concern and shall coordinate them within the Council, in accordance with the provisions of Article 102a.

Art. 103.2. The Council shall, acting by a qualified majority on a recommendation from the Commission, formulate a draft for the broad guidelines of the economic policies of the Member States and of the Community, and shall report its findings to the European Council.

Art. 103.A.1. Without prejudice to any other procedures provided for in this Treaty, the Council may, acting unanimously on a proposal from the Commission, decide upon the measures appropriate to the economic situation, in particular if severe difficulties arise in the supply of certain products.

Art. 103.A.2. Where a Member State is in difficulties or is seriously threatened with severe difficulties caused by exceptional occurrences beyond its control, the Council may, acting unanimously on a proposal from the Commission, grant, under certain conditions, Community financial assistance to the Member State concerned. Where the severe difficulties are caused by natural disasters, the Council shall act by qualified majority. The President of the Council shall inform the European Parliament of the decision taken.

Art. 3A.2. Concurrently with the foregoing, and as provided in this Treaty and in accordance with the timetable and the procedures set out therein, these activities shall include the irrevocable fixing of exchange rates leading to the introduction of a single currency, the ECU, and the definition and conduct of a single monetary policy and exchange rate policy the primary objective of both of which shall be to maintain price stability and, without prejudice to this objective, to support the general economic policies in the Community, in accordance with the principle of an open market economy with free competition.

### Creation and objectives of the European System of Central Banks (ESCB) and of the European Central Bank (ECB)

Art. 4.A. A European System of Central Banks (hereinafter referred to as 'ESCB') and a European Central Bank (hereinafter referred to as 'ECB') shall be established in accordance with the procedures laid down in this Treaty...

Art. 105.1. The primary objective of the ESCB shall be to maintain price stability. Without prejudice to the objective of price stability, the ESCB shall support the general economic policies in the Community with a view to contributing to the achievement of the objectives of the Community as laid down in Article 2.

*Art. 105.2. The basic tasks to be carried out through the ESCB shall be:*
- to define and implement the monetary policy of the Community;
- to conduct foreign exchange operations consistent with the provisions of Article 109;
- to hold and manage the official foreignreserves of the Member States;
- to promote the smooth operation of pament systems.

Art. 105.5. The ESCB shall contribute to the smooth conduct of policies pursued by the competent authorities relating to the prudential supervision of credit institutions and the stability of the financial system.

Art. 105.A.1. The ECB shall have the exclusive right to authorise the issue of banknotes within the Community. The ECB and the national central banks may issue such notes...

Art. 105.A.2. Member States may issue coins subject to approval by the ECB of the volume of the issue.

### Institutional Provisions
Monetary Committee

Art. 109.C. 1. In order to promote coordination of the policies of Member States to the full extent needed for the functioning of the internal market, a Monetary Committee with advisory status is hereby set up.

*It shall have the following tasks:*
- to keep under review the monetary and financial situation of the Member States and of the Community and the general payments system of the Member States and to report regularly thereon to the Council and to the Commission;
- to deliver opinions at the request of the Council or of the Commission, or on its own initiative for submission to those institutions;
- to contribute to the preparation of the work of the Council;
- to examine, at least once a year, the situation regarding the movement of capital and the freedom of payments, as they result from the application of this Treaty and of measures adopted by the Council; the examination shall cover all measures relating to capital movements and payments;the Committee shall report to the Commission and to the Council on the outcome of this examination.

The Member States and the Commission shall each appoint two members of the Monetary Committee.

Art. 109.C.2. At the start of the third stage, an Economic and Financial Committee shall be set up. The Monetary Committee provided for in paragraph 1 shall be dissolved.

### Transitory Dispositions

Art. 109.E.1. The second stage for achieving Economic and Monetary Union shall begin on 1 January 1994.

*European Monetary Institute (EMI)*

Art. 109.F.1. At the start of the second stage, a European Monetary Institute (hereinafter referred to as EMI) shall be established and take up its duties...

Art. 109.F.2. The EMI shall:
- strengthen the coordination of the monetary policies of the Member States, with the aim of ensuring price stability;
- monitor the functioning of the European Monetary System;
- facilitate the use of the ECU and oversee its development, including the smooth functioning of the ECU clearing system.

Art. 109.F.3. For the preparation of the third stage, the EMI shall:
- prepare the instruments and the procedures necessary for carrying out a single monetary policy in the third stage;
- supervise the technical preparation of ECU banknotes.

## Transitional provisions
*Convergence Criteria (1)*

Art. 109.J.1. The Commission and the EMI shall report to the Council on the progress made in the fulfilment by the Member States of their obligations regarding the achievement of Economic and Monetary Union. These reports shall include an examination of the compatibility between each Member State's national legislation, including the statutes of its national central bank, and Articles 107 and 108 of this Treaty and the Statute of the ESCB. The reports shall also examine the achievement of a high degree of sustainable convergence by reference to the fulfilment by each Member State of the following criteria:
- achievement of a high degree of price stability; this will be apparent from a rate of inflation which is close to that of, at most, the three best performing Member States in terms of price stability;
- the sustainability of the government financial position; this will be apparent from having achieved a government budgetary position without a deficit that is excessive as determined in accordance with Article 104.C.6;
- the observance of the normal fluctuation margins provided for by the exchange rate mechanism of the European Monetary System, for at least two years, without devaluing against the currency of any other Member State;
- the durability of convergence achieved by the Member State and of its participation in the exchange rate mechanism of the European Monetary System being reflected in the long term interest rate levels.

The four criteria mentioned in this paragraph and the relevant periods over which they are to be respected are developed further in a Protocol annexed to this Treaty. The reports of the Commission and the EMI shall also take account of the development of the ECU...

## Transitional provisions
*Convergence Criteria (2)*

Art. 104.C.2. The Commission shall monitor the development of the budgetary situation and of the stock of government debt in the Member States with a view to identifying gross errors. In particular it shall examine compliance with budgetary discipline on the basis of the following two criteria:
- whether the ratio of the planned or actual government deficit to gross domestic product exceeds a reference value, unless...
- whether the ratio of government debt to gross domestic product exceeds a reference value, unless the ratio is sufficiently diminishing and approaching the reference value at a satisfactory pace.

Art. 104.C.6. The Council shall, acting by a qualified majority on a recommendation from the Commission, and having considered any observations which the Member State concerned may wish to make, decide after an overall assessment whether an excessive deficit exists.

## Period

Art. 109.J.3. concerns the possible start of Phase III in 1997.

Art. 109.J.4. If by the end of 1997 the date for the beginning of the third stage has not been set, the third stage shall start on 1 January 1999. Before 1 July 1998, the Council, meeting in the composition of the Heads of State or Government, after a repetition of the procedure provided for in paragraphs 1 and 2, with the exception of the second indent of paragraph 2, taking into account the reports referred to in paragraph 1 and the opinion of the European Parliament, shall, acting by a qualified majority and on the basis of the recommendations of the Council referred to in paragraph 2, confirm which Member States fulfil the necessary conditions for the adoption of a single currency.

## Transitional provisions
### Exchange rates

Art. 109.G. The currency composition of the ECU basket shall not be changed. From the start of the third stage, the value of the ECU shall be irrevocably fixed in accordance with Article 109 L.4.

Art. 102.L.2. As soon as the ECB is established, it shall, if necessary, take over tasks of the EMI.
Art. 102.L.4. At the starting date of the third stage, the Council shall, acting with the unanimity of the Member States without a derogation, on a proposal from the Commission and after consulting the ECB, adopt the conversion rates at which their currencies shall be irrevocably fixed and at which irrevocably fixed rate the ECU shall be substituted for these currencies, and the ECU will become a currency in its own right. This measure shall by itself not modify the external value of the ECU. The Council shall, acting according to the same procedure, also take the other measures necessary for the rapid introduction of the ECU as the single currency of those Member States.

Art. 102.L.5. If it is decided ... to abrogate a derogation, the Council shall, acting with the unanimity of the Member States without a derogation and the Member State concerned, on a proposal from the Commission and after consulting the ECB, adopt the rate at which the ECU shall be substituted for the currency of the Member State concerned, and take the other measures necessary for the introduction of the ECU as the single currency in the Member State concerned.

### Member States benefiting from a derogation

Art. 109.K.2. At least once every two years, or at the request of a Member State with a derogation, the Commission and the ECB shall report to the Council ... After consulting the European Parliament and after discussion in the Council, meeting in the composition of the Heads of State or Government, the Council shall, acting by a qualified majority on a proposal from the Commission, decide which Member States with a derogation fulfil the necessary conditions on the basis of the criteria set out in Article 109.J.1., and abrogate the derogations of the Member States concerned.

# *a*ppendix **4**
## *Glossary*[3]

Terms other than "money" are classified by alphabetical order in 3 main categories:

a. financial terms
b. international institutions, and
c. personalities and international agreements.

Regarding international institutions, those created specifically for EMU and described in the articles of the Treaty of Union (see appendix 3), are not repeated in the glossary. These include, notably, the European Monetary Institute (EMI), the European Central Bank (ECB), the European System of Central Banks (ESCB) and the Monetary Committee.

## Money

Money originated as rare and sought-after objects (cattle, shells), and later as pieces of metal, which were used as a means of payment in the sale and purchase of goods instead of barter. Later, money became an instrument of settlement in general (including in financial transactions). Thus, money began to serve as a measure of value in exchanges. In this way the roles of money - unit of account, store of value (for savings) and lastly, means of payment - developed over time.

In modern society, metallic money co-exists with fiduciary money (from Latin, fides, confidence) and scriptural money. Metallic money, that is to say money whose value is determined by its metal content, also has a numismatic value for collectors. Fiduciary money refers to notes issued by banks with the authorisation of the "sovereign" whose monetary power is set against a store of precious metal - also called "cover" - in his coffers.

The development of commercial and financial exchanges led to an enormous increase in the demand for money. The "cover", also referred to as collateral or reserves, behind the issue of notes and coin also had to be increased, but the increase in reserves failed to keep pace with the growing volume of transactions. Moreover, it became apparent that a 100 % reserve ratio was not essential to maintain confidence on the part of holders of money. In this way the practice of issuing notes, without an equivalent cover of precious metal, was established.

The decline in reserve ratios continued with the development of scriptural money: cheques, credit cards, deposits, bank credits, etc.

Today, the differences between types of money have faded: term deposits, savings deposits, treasury certificates...are examples of savings or investment instruments. However, it is still essential that money be supported by an efficient financial network and that it have a lender of last resort i.e. a central bank that guarantees its value.

3. Sources: "Lexique de banque et de bourse", Sousi-Roubi, B., 2nd edition, Dalloz, 1986
   "Au service de l'Union européenne: Guide du citoyen sur le fonctionnement des institutions de l'Union européenne" ISBN92-77-93106-X, Edition 1986
   "Lexique des termes économiques et financiers", Comité national de l'épargne mobilière, Editor J. Craps, 1960

Financial Terms

| Financial Terms | Definition |
| --- | --- |
| Asymmetric shocks | Transitory imbalance between two regions arising from a sharp change in economic conditions. For example, the collapse in the steel industry resulted in unemployment blackspots in steel-producing regions. |
| Balance of payments | Measure (in money terms) of the inflow and outflow of goods and capital of a country. If one adds to the balance of trade (the difference between goods imported and those exported) services (transport, insurance) and foreign payments (inward, such as revenue from overseas investments and outward, such as transfers by immigrants to their countries of origin), one obtains the balance of payments on current account. |
| Buying rate | Exchange rate at which banks purchase a currency. Central bank purchases to support a currency are also at this rate. |
| Central bank | Institution playing the role of banker's bank and conducting monetary policy. Usually, the lender of last resort for a currency. |
| Central exchange rates | Exchange rate normally situated mid-way between the buying and selling rates. |
| Clearing | The process by which reciprocal obligations are settled (cf. "settlement") |
| Convertibility | The capability of a currency to be exchanged against gold or another currency. In 1971, the abandonment of dollar convertibility against gold marked the start of a period of monetary instability which led Europeans to create their own monetary system. |
| Euro- and euro | Used as a prefix, euro-... refers to a currency held in a bank installed in a country other than that which issued the currency. Therefore, euro-dollars is the name given to dollar denominated securities held outside the United States, whether in Europe or elsewhere. It is estimated that 60% of U.S. money is held by non-Americans. The prefix euro here has nothing to do with Europe.<br>Used on its own, euro signifies European currency.<br>(One single exception: eurocent). |
| Exchange rate | This is the price of one currency against another. See "buying rate" or "selling rate". |
| Executive prerogative | Any right conferred upon the executive authority of a country such as, for example, the right to coin money. It follows that all matters relating to money are the responsibility of powers beyond the influence of ordinary citizens who, as a result, take little interest in monetary affairs or consider them wholly bound to decisions taken by the relevant authorities. |

| Fiduciary money | Banknotes and coins. Their value depends upon continued confidence in the issuer, usually a central bank. |
|---|---|
| Floating of currencies | Currency floating occurs when there are no restrictions on exchange rate fluctuations. In such a situation, fixed exchange rates, tunnels and snakes are abandoned. A distinction can be made between strong currencies, which appreciate in relation to others, and weak currencies, which depreciate on a regular basis. Daily variations in exchange rates can be considerable. These fluctuations, and even more so, alignment or currencies, are considered a hindrance to international trade. Misalignments happen when, for some reason or another, official exchange rates do not reflect the actual strength of the currency in terms of the competitivity of the economy it represents. A currency is defined as stable in external terms, when variations in its exchange rate against the principal international reference currencies remain limited. |
| Gross Domestic Product (GDP) | Value of wealth created in a year within a country. GDP denotes a country's economic strength. |
| Hegemony | Supremacy of one state or nation in an international system. Hegemonic stability theory argues that members of the international monetary system seek the leadership of a single country or a single central bank as the best guarantee of equilibrium. |
| Inflation | Tendency for the price of goods and services to increase. When there is high inflation, money "loses value" because the same amount buys less in the future than today. Low inflation preserves a currency's intrinsic value, known as its internal stability. |
| Issuers of notes and coin | Institutions whose entire capital is held by the state which accords them the sole right to issue legal money: notes and coin. Generally, these institutions are central banks. |
| Legal tender | Term applied to a means of payment that one is obliged to accept at its face value (that which is inscribed on the note or coin). Notes and coins of a country's currency have legal tender in that country, since all parties are legally obliged to accept them. This is not the case with foreign currency. |
| Lender of last resort | Role played by the central bank when it lends to banks to increase their liquidity or, exceptionally, to prevent a snowballing series of bankruptcies in the sector. |
| Liquidity | Assets which are easily converted into cash: current accounts, savings accounts etc. |
| Margin of fluctuation | The limit put on a currency's variation in relation to its reference point/currency. |

| | |
|---|---|
| Means of payment | The chosen method, defined by law or by custom, for making payment for goods or for settling debts. Normally, the chosen method is money, but other methods are used from time to time. |
| Monetary reform | Monetary reform is the replacement of the existing monetary standard or basis by a new one. It is similar to the decimalization in the UK and Ireland. Thus, the introduction of the euro is not a monetary reform. |
| Monetary "snake" | Narrow fluctuation limits within a range of limits or tunnel of fluctuation. European snake also used to distinguish the stricter fluctuation limits imposed on currencies participating in the European Monetary System (based on bilaterally agreed margins between those taking part) from those applied to currencies within the international tunnel of fluctuation (based on wider margins established for all participating currencies against the dollar). |
| National debt | Total national debt arising from the accumulation of public sector deficits over the years. |
| Overdraft | A credit that a bank grants to a client authorising him to overdraw his account for an agreed amount and period of time. |
| Parity | Official value of the currency of a country in relation to a reference base. In the EMS, the parity of EU currencies is defined in relation to the ecu. In current practice, this term also means "exchange rate", although the latter fluctuates in accordance with market forces. |
| Protectionism | Commercial policy that gives preference to national goods and services over imports, and achieved through customs tariffs or other administrative barriers. |
| Public sector deficit | Difference between public receipts and expenditure. Generally expressed as a % of GDP. |
| Reserve funds | Each bank must maintain at the central bank a sum proportional to deposits received or credits granted. Reserves also comprise gold or foreign currency held by the central bank, in every State to meet foreign payment obligations. |
| Scriptural money or book-currency | Money which allows transfers between accounts by simple act of signature: credit cards, cheques, or bank payment orders etc. This is money which is payable in the short-term. |
| Seigniorage | Governments have "sovereignty" in issuance of notes and government bonds. If a government inflates the economy by 10%, then the debt it issues in that currency may be worth 10 % less and it has the possibility of repaying the debt in a currency depreciated by inflation. This additional government income at the expense of ordinary citizens is known as "seigniorage". |

| | |
|---|---|
| Selling rate | Exchange rate at which banks sell a currency. Central bank sales to limit currency appreciation are also at this rate. |
| Settlement | Payments made to close two reciprocal obligations up to the limit of the smaller amount. The English term "clearing" is more often used. The currency obligations of a country are "cleared" by transfers between central banks. |
| Store of value | Accumulating wealth or savings. Can be hoarded (under the mattress) or invested to gain interest (savings accounts). Banks play an important redistributive role, transferring surpluses built up through savings to those able to create wealth via investment projects. |
| Structural adjustment | Radical change in the type of management of a society, often to reduce the role of the public sector. |
| System of mutual credit | Credit is the exchange of a good, money, for example, against a promise of future payment. Thus credit exists when the benefits of the two parties are dissociated in time. "Time" is the determinant factor. There is a system of mutual credit, or network between banks which provide credit to each other. |
| Tunnel of fluctuation | For the currencies which take part, the tunnel determines limits currencies may fluctuate. Central banks must buy a currency which is too weak or sell a currency which is too strong in the foreign exchange markets to maintain the rates within the limits. |
| Unit of account | Unit of reference in a transaction between two or more parties. In contrast to money which circulates between the parties, a unit of account does not necessarily possess the means of payment function. It represents the "standard" value of money. |
| Value of a currency | Because money is a specific form of asset, it has a value. The value of money is established relative to that of other goods: it is represented by a certain purchasing power. If the price of goods rises, it is because the value of money declines: with the same unit of money, one can buy less. The change in the value of a monetary unit is represented in indexes showing price movements, i.e. inflation. The stability of a currency determines its capacity to maintain its value in relation to the price of goods, but also in relation to other currencies. |
| (Face) value of currency | Face value is that indicated on notes or coins. |

*International institutions*

| Name | Definition |
|------|------------|
| Bank for International Settlements (BIS) | The BIS was created in 1930 to carry out plans on the basis of reparations due from Germany, and more generally to assist relations between central banks. Today it holds a pre-eminent position in the system of international monetary cooperation. It is at the centre of the ecu settlement system. Headquarters: Basle. |
| Council of Economic and Finance Ministers (ECOFIN) | Ministers of Finance or Economics of Member States meet regularly (ECOFIN Council) to decide on common financial and monetary questions. They also do the preparatory work for decisions by the European Council and will be responsible for recommending the exchange rate of the euro "vis à vis" other international currencies. |
| Council of the Euro | Created in December 1997. Non-decision making body composed of one EC representative and of the Ministers for Economy and Finance of the EMU Member States responsible for elaborating the economic policies of these States. |
| Council of the European Union | Better known as "Council of Ministers". Meeting in Council, Member States legislate for the Union, fix its political objectives, coordinate national policies and sort out internal differences or those with other institutions. The Council's legitimacy resides in its composition: ministers who are answerable to their national parliaments and public opinion. It is an institution that is both supranational and inter-governmental: each Member State takes turns to assume the presidency for a 6-month period. |
| Economic and Financial Committee (EFC) | Has taken over the responsibilities from the former Monetary Committee as from January 1999. |
| Ecu Banking Association (EBA) | The EBA was founded in Paris in 1985 by 18 commercial banks and the EIB (see below). Its principal mission was the development and daily management of the ECU settlement system. The 101 current EBA members comprise banks from all EU Member States as well as Australia, the U.S. , Japan and Switzerland. Almost half have Settlement Bank status and participate directly in the ecu settlement system. The EBA's action is inherently linked to the extension and utilisation of the euro, in close collaboration with the EMI and the EU central banks. |
| European Central Bank (ECB) | Created by the Treaty on European Union in 1992. Together with the national central banks, it makes up the European System of Central Banks, established in the third phase of EMU and an integral part of it since 1 January 1999. The Treaty guarantees the independence of the ECB and the national central banks. The ECB's task is to watch over the internal stability of the euro and to implement the exchange rate policy as given by the Economic and Financial Committee. Head Office: Frankfurt. |

| | |
|---|---|
| European Coal and Steel Community (ECSC) | A common market for coal and steel created by the ECSC Treaty - or Treaty of Paris - for a period of 50 years in April 1951. The ECSC's goal was to test a formula which could be extended gradually from coal and steel into other areas, so that through various sectors of activity, a Europe-wide policy could be constructed. |
| European Commission (EC), current abbreviation for the Commission of the European Communities (CEC) | Forerunner, together with the EU Council, of the European executive. The European Commission proposes legislation (directives) which are then subject to the approval of the Council and Parliament. The Commission is the guardian of the treaties as well as the body which executes the Union's policies and has responsibility for its international commercial relations. Generally, the Commission is the motor of the European integration process. It comprises 20 Commissioners and 15 000 personnel. Headquarters: Brussels |
| European Investment Bank (EIB) | The EIB, created in 1957 by the Treaty of Rome, is the European Union's financing institution. It grants long-term loans to investment projects that contribute towards the balanced development and integration of the Union. With annual loans of 29.5 billion euro, it is one of the top international financing institutions. It has over 900 employees. Headquarters: Luxembourg |
| European Monetary Cooperation Fund (EMCF) | Established in 1973, it derived from the Committee of Governors which was formed in 1964. The EMCF's powers were too diluted to allow it to constitute a robust platform for the development of a Monetary Union in Europe. Precursor of the EMI and the ECB. |
| European Parliament | The European Parliament, the world's biggest multinational assembly elected by direct universal suffrage, is the democratic expression of the political will of the peoples of the European Union. It maintains close relations with national parliaments. It shares power with the Council. Its 626 members are elected for 5 years. Last elections: 1999. Headquarters: Strasbourg, Luxembourg and Brussels. Has important budgetary powers. |
| International Monetary Fund (IMF) | Created at Bretton Woods, the objective of the IMF (located in Washington D.C.) was, until 1970, the stabilisation of exchange rates and the convertibility of currencies. The IMF has become a permanent forum for the exchange of views where problems are resolved through consultation among member countries thereby avoiding persistent disputes. To increase international monetary reserves, the IMF issues Special Drawing Rights (SDRs). These are international units of account which have, however, never acquired the monetary character of the ecu. Conscious of the numerous problems still outstanding, the participants in the Bretton Woods Conference created the International Bank for Reconstruction and Development (IBRD), also known as the World Bank. The latter's initial role to finance the reconstruction of war devastated Europe and to develop the Third World was extended to |

| | |
|---|---|
| | assisting world development. |
| Monetary Committee | See Economic and Financial Committee (EFC) |
| Organisation for Economic Cooperation and Development (OECD) | The convention for Economic Cooperation and Development signed in Paris in December 1960 enters into force on 30.09.1961, giving birth to the OECD, thus succeeding to the European Organisation for Economic Cooperation (EOEC) created in 1948. The aim of the OECD, after the second world-war, is to set up a cooperation programme to rebuild Europe with the help of the USA. OECD's role consists of promoting economic and social welfare within its member countries helping their governments to formulate and coordinate their policies ; it must also stimulate efforts made in order to help developing countries. The EC also takes part in its activities. |
| SWIFT (Society for Worldwide Interbank Financial Telecommunication) | This is a non-profit company incorporated under Belgian law in 1973 whose capital is held by 3000 banks. Its services to financial institutions cover the handling and communication of financial data and computer programmes used in monetary, property and commercial transactions. Its employs 1200 people. Headquarters: Brussels |
| TARGET | Trans-European Automated Real-time Gross Settlement Transfer. This is an international system whereby large sums in euro are settled. Its cost will probably limit its usage to central and international banks. |

*Personalities and International Agreements*

| Name | Definition |
|---|---|
| Raymond Barre (1924 - (Barre plan) | Mayor of Lyons since 1995. Born at Saint-Denis, Réunion (F). Civil servant and international politician. Professor of law and economic science. Vice-President of the EC 1967-72. Prime Minister of France 1976-78. |
| François Bilger (1934 - | Professor at the Pasteur University, Strasbourg, Faculty of Economic and Management Sciences |
| Bretton Woods Agreement | A conference held at Bretton Woods (New-Hampshire in the USA) in July 1944 decided the basis of a new international monetary system which lasted until 1971. This system was founded on fixed exchange rates around the dollar, at that time convertible into gold. It was supervised by the IMF, with the World Bank responsible for providing aid to poorer countries. The conference did not take up some of the ideas of Maynard Keynes (UK) who proposed the creation of a world currency (Bancor), issued by an international bank. The Bretton Woods Conference achieved the majority of its medium-term objectives but the limited nature of the reforms proposed - the international monetary system was centred on the balance of payments situation in the USA - made it inevitable that problems would re-emerge in the long-term. |

| | |
|---|---|
| Umberto Colombo (1927 - | Italian entrepreneur, born at Livorno. Attended Universities of Pavia and Massachusetts Institute of Technology. Director of Montedison. President of the Italian Agency of Atomic Energy. President of the European Scientific Foundation. Minister 1993-94. Several scientific publications. |
| Jacques Delors (1925 - | French politician and economist, born in Paris. University of Paris. Socialist party. Departmental director, Banque de France 1945-62. Minister of the Economy and Finance 1981-84. President of the European Commission 1985-94. |
| Willem Frederik Duisenberg (1935 - | Dutch economist born in Heerenveen (NL). State University of Groningen; IMF 1966-69; Finance Minister 1973-77; President of the Bank for International Settlements (BIS) 1988-90 ; 1994-97; President of the EMI 1994-97; President of the BCE since January 1999. Publications: "Le FMI et le Système Monétaire International 1966". |
| Valéry Giscard d'Estaing (1926 - | French politician and civil servant, born at Koblenz (D). Ecole Polytechnique and Ecole Nationale d'Administration (ENA). President of the French Republic 1974-81. Minister of Financial and Economic Affairs 1962-66, 1969-74. |
| Jean-Pierre Fourcade (1929 - (Fourcade Report) | French politician, born at Marmande (F). Law faculty, Institute of political studies. Ecole Nationale d'Administration (ENA). Minister of the Economy and Finance 1974-76, Minister 1976-77, Mayor of Saint-Cloud 1973-89. |
| Hans Dietrich Genscher (1927 - | German politician, born at Reideburg (D). Free Democratic Party (FDP). Federal Minister 1969-92. Vice-Chancellor 1974-92. Honorary doctorates from many universities. |
| Paul de Grauwe (1946 - | Belgian economist and politician born in Brussels (B). Catholic University of Louvain (where he teaches). John Hopkins University. Member of the Belgian Parliament. |
| Michael Geuenich | German trades union federation. |
| Klaus Hänsch (1938 - | President of the European Parliament 1994-96. |
| Fredrich August von Hayek (1899-1992) | Born in Vienna. Economist at the London School of Economics with degrees in law and sociology. Specialist in monetary economics and economic growth. His analysis of political systems led him to favour those which allow the free play of market forces. He obtained the Nobel prize for economics in 1974. |
| Philippe Herzog (1940 | Born at Bruay-en-Artois (Pas de Calais), France. Graduate of ENSAE, Master of economics. Elected 18 June 1989 to European Parliament. Formerly responsible for economic questions in the French Communist Party. Professor at University of Paris X. |

| Jean-Claude Juncker (1954 - | Prime Minister of the Grand Duchy of Luxembourg since 1995. Born at Redange (L). Member of Christian Social Party. Actively participated in drafting the Treaty of Union and instrumental in obtaining a favourable outcome to the Dublin Summit in December 1996. |
|---|---|
| Helmut Kohl (1930 - | Born at Ludwigshafen. Studied law, political science and history. In 1973 became president of the Christian Democratic Party (CDU). Chancellor 1982 - 98. Architect of German reunification. |
| Alexandre Lamfalussy (1929 - | Belgian banker, born at Kapuvar (H). Economist, bank director. Counsellor, Vice-President then Director-General of the BIS 1976-93. President of the EMI 1994 to June 1997. Replaced by the Dutch central banker, Mr Willem Duisenberg. |
| Marshall Plan | Aid plan, financed by the U.S., for the reconstruction of the European economy after the Second World War. Named after the American general who, following the war, became Secretary of the State Department 1947-49. |
| Jean Monnet (1888 - 1979) | Together with Robert Schuman, one of the fathers of European integration. Economist and industrialist born in Cognac (F). He managed the international affairs of the family business, and in 1917 participated in the creation of the allied council on maritime transport. This convinced him that only solidarity between European nations would enable them to restore their economic strength and international esteem. Several countries asked for his help in redressing their finances. Author of the "Schuman Plan", basis of the European integration process. First president of the ECSC. He called for European integration to be accelerated and notably for the introduction of a supranational authority. |
| Robert Alexander Mundell (1932 - | Economist. Winner of the Nobel Prize in 1999. Born in Kingston, Ontario. Ph.D. Candian Professor of Economics at the Massachusetts Institute of Technology. Jacques Rueff prize and medal in 1983. Known for his work on optimal monetary zones. Recommended the European Monetary Union in 1969. Also called the "godfather" of the euro. |
| John Pinder (1924 - | Born in London (UK). President of the Federal Trust, Honorary President of the Union of European Federalists (UEF), Vice-President of the International European Mouvement and Deputy Chairman of the European Mouvement in the United Kingdom. He regularly teaches at the "Collège d'Europe" in Bruges and, for 21 years, has been Director of the Institute for Policy Studies in London. Recent publications: "European Community: The Building of a Union (1991)"; " Federal Union: the Pioneers (avec R. Mayne, 1990)"; " Maastricht and Beyond (1994)". |
| Alain Prate (1928 - 1997) | Born at Lille (F). Director-General of Economic and Financial Affairs at the EC, 1961-65. Economic adviser to General de Gaulle 1967-69. Vice-President of the EIB 1984-94. President of the board of advisers of "CNP Assurances". Author of the book "Quelle Europe?" (published by Julliard). |

| | |
|---|---|
| Romano Prodi<br>(1939 - | President of the Commission 1999. Born in Scandiano, Italy. Catholic University of Milan, degree in law; London School of Economics, post-graduate studies. Minister of Industry 1978 - 79. Chairman IRI 1982 - 89, 1993 - 94. Chairman Ulivo Party 1995. Prime Minister 1996 - 98. Member of Parliament 1996 - 99. |
| Christa Randzio-Plath<br>(1940 - | Born in Germany. Head, since 1992, of the Monetary Affairs Sub-committee of the European Parliament. Doctorate in law and sociology. Author of numerous articles. |
| Jacques Rueff<br>(1896 - 1978) | Born in Paris. Student at the Ecole Polytechnique, doctorate in law. Author of many reports on the FRC which he helped to revive. It was on the basis of one of these reports that President de Gaulle established the new franc. Member of the financial section of the League of Nations 1927-30. In 1952, he was nominated to the Court of Justice of the ECSC. In denouncing the hegemony of the USD, he remained until his death an ardent defender of the return to the gold standard. |
| Jacques Santer<br>(1937 - | Luxembourg politician, born at Wasserbillig (L). Universities of Strasbourg and Paris. Lawyer. Christian Social Party. Minister of Finance 1979-84. Prime Minister up to 1994. President of the Commission 1994 - 99. |
| Helmut Schmidt<br>(1918 - | Economist and German politician born in Hamburg. Social Democrat. Minister 1969-74 and Federal Chancellor 1974-82. |
| Robert Schuman<br>(1886 - 1963) | With Jean Monnet, one of the fathers of European integration. Born in Luxembourg, he studied law at German universities. Deputy for the Moselle from 1919. Minister of Finance, Minister of Foreign Affairs in France. On 9 May 1950, he gave the famous Salon de l'Horloge speech which announced the creation of the ECSC. Since then, the 9th of May has been celebrated as Europe day. He believed that the common Christian origin of several European leaders of the time would cement European unity. |
| Amartya Kumar Sen<br>(1933 - | Economist, winner of the Nobel Prize in 1998. Born in Dhaka, Bangladesh. Master at Trinity College, Cambridge. Teaches at Harvard University and at the Jadarpur University, Calcutta. Also professor in philosophy and political economy. Proponent of democracy and solidarity as fundamental principles of sound economics. Denounced the lack of consensus in the European monetary construction in his publication "Living as Equals", Clarendon Press, Oxford, 1996. |
| Yves-Thibault de Silguy<br>(1948 - | Student at Ecole Nationale d'Administration (ENA) 1974-76. Foreign Affairs Secretary in the EC Economic and Financial Affairs Directorate 1976-80, technical adviser with responsibility for European and international economic matters (cabinet of Prime Minister J. Chirac) 1986-88. EC Commissioner for Economic, Financial and Monetary affairs 1995-99. |

| | |
|---|---|
| Paul-Henri Spaak (1899 -1972) | Belgian politician. Born in Brussels. After 1936 he was several times Minister of foreign affairs and Prime Minister. In 1949, he was elected President of the Consultative Assembly of the Council of Europe and 1957 Secretary-General of NATO. Ardent defender of European integration, he launched in 1953 an appeal for European political union. It was under his direction that the group of representatives of the six Member States, called the "Spaak Committee", drafted the Treaty of Rome. |
| Alfred Steinherr (1944 - | Born in Germany. Studied mathematics in the U.S. Professor of economics and director at the EIB. EBA Vice-President. Numerous publications. |
| Hans Tietmeyer (1931 - | President of the Bundesbank since 1993. Born in Metelen (D). Worked at European Institutions and at the OECD. Minister of State 1982-89. Member of Governing Committee of the Bundesbank since 1990. |
| Leo Tindemans (1922 - (Rapport Tindemans) | Belgian politician. Born in Zwijndrecht (B). Prime Minister 1974-78. President of European Popular Party 1976-85. Member of European Parliament 1989-99. |
| Robert Triffin (1911 - 1995) | Economist known for his proposals for reforming the IMF (1961). These were rejected on various grounds, notably the loss of national sovereignty implied. Nonetheless, it was recognised that his ideas could be applied within the narrower context of the European Economic Community. Ardent proponent of a world currency and a supranational authority to assure the stability of an international monetary system. |
| Karl von Wogau (1941 - | Born in Germany. President of the Economic, Monetary and Industrial Policy Commission. Doctorate in law from INSEAD. Publication "Der Milliardenjoker". "Bundesverdienst Kreuz " - merit order of the Federal Republic of Germany. |
| Pierre Werner (1913 - (Werner Plan) | Born in Lille (F). Lawyer and Luxembourg politician. Prime Minister 1969-74 and 1979-84. Governor of the EIB 1958-84. President of the EC Economic Affairs Committee 1970-71. President of European Satellites Organisation. Various publications such as "Itinéraires Luxembourgeois et Européens - 1945-85". The Werner Plan was the first official expression of monetary integration in Europe. |
| Dr. Karl-Heinz Wessel (1927 - | President of the "Bundesverband Deutscher Banken". |
| Sir Nigel Wicks (1940 - | Civil servant. Graduate of Cambridge University. Later worked at IMF and International Bank for Reconstruction and Development (IBRD) or World Bank. Secretary to the Prime Minister. President of the Monetary Committee. Highly appreciated for his thoroughly European approach in the work of this committee which played a crucial role in the preparation for EMU. |

# *l*ist of questions

Why have convergence criteria:
(1) a necessary harmonisation of Member States' economic policies? . . . . . . . . . . . . . . . . . . . . . . . . . 27
(2) a reform of our society? . . . . . . . . . . . . . . . . . . . . . . . . . . . . . . . . . . . . . . . . . . . . . . . . . . . . 27
Why have the convergence criteria been criticised? . . . . . . . . . . . . . . . . . . . . . . . . . . . . . . . . . . . 27
Do all countries participate in EMU and what lies in store for those countries that did not join in 1999?. . . 28
What is the Council of the Euro? . . . . . . . . . . . . . . . . . . . . . . . . . . . . . . . . . . . . . . . . . . . . . . . . 29
Was there a risk that EMU might not take place or might be delayed? . . . . . . . . . . . . . . . . . . . . . . . 29
2. The symbolic importance of the euro . . . . . . . . . . . . . . . . . . . . . . . . . . . . . . . . . . . . . . . . . . . . **30**
What is the symbolic value of the euro and the philosophy behind it? . . . . . . . . . . . . . . . . . . . . . . . . 30
When was the name "euro" chosen to designate the single currency? . . . . . . . . . . . . . . . . . . . . . . . 30
Will the euro entail a loss of national sovereignty? . . . . . . . . . . . . . . . . . . . . . . . . . . . . . . . . . . . . 31
Will the single currency diminish our cultural identity?. . . . . . . . . . . . . . . . . . . . . . . . . . . . . . . . . . 32
3. Some concrete results . . . . . . . . . . . . . . . . . . . . . . . . . . . . . . . . . . . . . . . . . . . . . . . . . . . . . . **32**
What are the advantages of the euro for businesses? . . . . . . . . . . . . . . . . . . . . . . . . . . . . . . . . . 32
Is the euro compatible with asymmetric shocks? . . . . . . . . . . . . . . . . . . . . . . . . . . . . . . . . . . . . . 33
What will be the advantages of the euro for banks? . . . . . . . . . . . . . . . . . . . . . . . . . . . . . . . . . . . 33
Under EMU, who controls the banks? . . . . . . . . . . . . . . . . . . . . . . . . . . . . . . . . . . . . . . . . . . . . . 33
What are the advantages of the euro for the individual? . . . . . . . . . . . . . . . . . . . . . . . . . . . . . . . . 33
What are the advantages of the single currency for the economy? . . . . . . . . . . . . . . . . . . . . . . . . . 34
What is the international potential of the euro? . . . . . . . . . . . . . . . . . . . . . . . . . . . . . . . . . . . . . . . 34
What are the risks that EMU might fail? . . . . . . . . . . . . . . . . . . . . . . . . . . . . . . . . . . . . . . . . . . . 35
How does the single currency contribute to the stability of the international monetary system? . . . . . . . 36
Is the single currency not detrimental to employment? . . . . . . . . . . . . . . . . . . . . . . . . . . . . . . . . . 36
Will the euro be a strong currency? . . . . . . . . . . . . . . . . . . . . . . . . . . . . . . . . . . . . . . . . . . . . . . 37
4. The change-over from national currencies to euro. . . . . . . . . . . . . . . . . . . . . . . . . . . . . . . . . . . . **38**
How did the transition from ecu to euro take place? . . . . . . . . . . . . . . . . . . . . . . . . . . . . . . . . . . . 38
Will the single currency and national currencies circulate in parallel? . . . . . . . . . . . . . . . . . . . . . . . . 39
What happens to the currencies which do not participate at the start? . . . . . . . . . . . . . . . . . . . . . . . 39
What is the cost of transition to the single currency and who bears the cost? . . . . . . . . . . . . . . . . . . . 40
5. Some practical implications. . . . . . . . . . . . . . . . . . . . . . . . . . . . . . . . . . . . . . . . . . . . . . . . . . . **40**
What becomes of current contracts denominated in ecu or in national currency (continuity of contracts)?. 40
Are our monetary assets not depreciating in value? . . . . . . . . . . . . . . . . . . . . . . . . . . . . . . . . . . . 40
Ecu transaction costs were high. What happens with the euro? . . . . . . . . . . . . . . . . . . . . . . . . . . . 41
At what rates are national currencies converted into euro? . . . . . . . . . . . . . . . . . . . . . . . . . . . . . . . 41
How to round the converted amounts into euro?. . . . . . . . . . . . . . . . . . . . . . . . . . . . . . . . . . . . . . 41
6. The Euro after its launch . . . . . . . . . . . . . . . . . . . . . . . . . . . . . . . . . . . . . . . . . . . . . . . . . . . . . **42**
How has the euro performed on the financial markets? . . . . . . . . . . . . . . . . . . . . . . . . . . . . . . . . . 42
Has the increased transparency brought about by the euro affected consumer prices?. . . . . . . . . . . . . 42
How has the Euro evolved on the exchange markets? . . . . . . . . . . . . . . . . . . . . . . . . . . . . . . . . . . 42
Has the Euro impacted on economic growth and employment? . . . . . . . . . . . . . . . . . . . . . . . . . . . . 43
Why are crossborder payments complicated and expensive? . . . . . . . . . . . . . . . . . . . . . . . . . . . . . 43
Will crossborder transfers improve? . . . . . . . . . . . . . . . . . . . . . . . . . . . . . . . . . . . . . . . . . . . . . . 44
How does one understand the new prices of goods? . . . . . . . . . . . . . . . . . . . . . . . . . . . . . . . . . . . 44
What has been the evolution on the political front?. . . . . . . . . . . . . . . . . . . . . . . . . . . . . . . . . . . . 44
7. ...and in 2002 . . . . . . . . . . . . . . . . . . . . . . . . . . . . . . . . . . . . . . . . . . . . . . . . . . . . . . . . . . . . **45**
What will our wallets contain in 2002? . . . . . . . . . . . . . . . . . . . . . . . . . . . . . . . . . . . . . . . . . . . . 45
What security measures are taken to protect against falsification of the euro? . . . . . . . . . . . . . . . . . . 45
Are bank notes identifiable by people with impaired sight? . . . . . . . . . . . . . . . . . . . . . . . . . . . . . . . 45
Do the coins contain metals such as nickel which can provoke allergies?. . . . . . . . . . . . . . . . . . . . . . 45
Who needs to prepare for the single currency? . . . . . . . . . . . . . . . . . . . . . . . . . . . . . . . . . . . . . . 45

# $\mathcal{R}$ecommended reading

*In French*

- "Monnaie, monnaies", Michèle Giacobbi and Anne-Marie Gronier, Le Monde Poche Editions, Marabout No. 8610, 1994

- "L'Europe racontée aux jeunes", Jacques Le Goff and Charley Case, Edition du Seuil, 1996

*In English*

- "User Guide to the Euro", Editors G. Bishop, J. Perez and S. van Tuyll - Publisher: Sweet & Maxwell, 1996

- "Everything you always wanted to ask about the Euro... and were afraid to ask!", Lyndon HARRISON MEP, S.C. Printing Ltd., 1997

*In Spanish*

- "La UEM en entredicho", Emilio Ontiveros and Francisco José Valero, Encuentro Ediciones OIKOS NOMOS, 1996

- "Guía Práctica Unión Europea: Respuesta a 50 de las preguntas que los ciudadanos españoles nos hacemos sobre el Tratado de Maastricht", Daniel de Busturia, CDN, 1993

*In German, English, Danish, French, Greek, Italian, Dutch and Swedish*

- "Europe. . .Questions and answers - When will we have euros in our pockets?"

Published by the Office of Official Publications of the European Communities, Luxembourg 1996

# *i*ndex

# Financing Europe's Future

The European Investment Bank (EIB), the European Union's financing institution, is helping to build a closer-knit and more united Europe.

Through its lending operations, it provides long-term finance for capital projects fulfilling the European Union's objectives:

- fostering the development of the less favoured regions;
- improving communications;
- protecting the environment;
- enhancing the competitiveness of industry and small and medium-sized enterprises.

Under its Amsterdam Special Action Programme, the EIB has expanded its financing operations to include the education and health sectors and innovative SMEs, thereby contributing towards meeting the challenges facing our societies.

Outside the Union, the EIB participates in development aid and cooperation policies in support of more than 120 countries.

**European Investment Bank**

*The European Union's financing institution*

100, boulevard Konrad Adenauer   L-2950 Luxembourg
Tel (+352) 43 79-1   Fax (+352) 43 77 04
Internet  www.eib.org

 **romeuro**

Since its creation in 1990, the non-profit seeking PROMEURO, association of citizens for the promotion of the European currency, works to involve citizens in the preparation of the Economic and Monetary Union. Only with this participation, will this ambitious programme elicit the solidarity among participants necessary to its success.

*Its statutes state:*

The Association PROMEURO was born out of the Comity for the promotion of the ecu created in 1987 by the Group of the European Institutions of the Union of European Federalists (UEF). Its objective is to prepare the European consumers for their common currency by stimulating its use there where it offers comparative advantages. The Association settles all its payments in ecus/euros. (Art.1).

The association is independent from political and religious allegiance. It can join and co-operate with other groups with similar aims or offering the professional services judged necessary for its achievements.

*PROMEURO's Board of Directors comprises*

Jean-Jacques SCHUL (President) - European Investment Bank

Vittorio Cidone (Vice-President) - retired from the European Commission

Christian Glöckner - Inter Regional Institute (IRI)

Fabio Morvilli (Treasurer) - Société Financière des Télécommunications (SOFTE)

Max Osterrieth - Banker and consultant

Hubert de Viron - EPEC

*Its Honorary Committee comprises*

Daniel de Busturia, President Grupo Estrategias de Empresa

Viscount Etienne Davignon, President Association for European Monetary Union (AEMU)

Fernand Herman, European Parliamentarian

Jean-Claude Juncker, Prime Minister Luxembourg

Matti Korhonen, Member of the Board Central Bank of Finland

Luis Marti, Vice-President European Investment Bank

Mario Monti, Member of the European Commission

Ariane Obolensky, Honorary Vice-President European Investment Bank

Wolfgang Roth, Vice-President European Investment Bank

Sir Brian Unwin, Honorary President European Investment Bank

Eric Vaes, INVESTOR Brussels

Karel van Miert, Member of the European Commission

Pierre Werner, Honorary State Minister of Luxembourg

Dr. Karel von Wogau, European Parliamentarian

PROMEURO has representations in various countries of the European Union.

*For further information*

PROMEURO Ltd.

1 Avenue de la Gare, L-1611 Luxembourg

Telephone : (352) 48 55 06

Fax : (352) 40 41 61

*Finally, PROMEURO thanks the following sponsors:*

The European Commission

The European Investment Bank

SOFTE